$\mathcal{P}$ROFILES IN
WORLD HISTORY

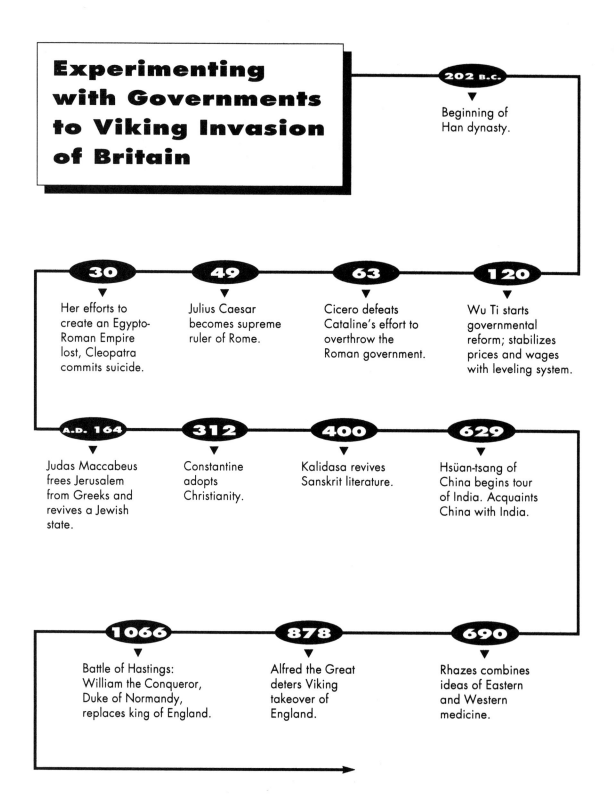

Experimenting with Governments to Viking Invasion of Britain

202 B.C.
Beginning of Han dynasty.

30
Her efforts to create an Egypto-Roman Empire lost, Cleopatra commits suicide.

49
Julius Caesar becomes supreme ruler of Rome.

63
Cicero defeats Cataline's effort to overthrow the Roman government.

120
Wu Ti starts governmental reform; stabilizes prices and wages with leveling system.

A.D. 164
Judas Maccabeus frees Jerusalem from Greeks and revives a Jewish state.

312
Constantine adopts Christianity.

400
Kalidasa revives Sanskrit literature.

629
Hsüan-tsang of China begins tour of India. Acquaints China with India.

1066
Battle of Hastings: William the Conqueror, Duke of Normandy, replaces king of England.

878
Alfred the Great deters Viking takeover of England.

690
Rhazes combines ideas of Eastern and Western medicine.

PROFILES IN WORLD HISTORY

Significant Events and the People

Who Shaped Them

2

Experimenting with Governments to Viking Invasion of Britain

JOYCE MOSS

and

GEORGE WILSON

AN IMPRINT OF GALE RESEARCH
AN INTERNATIONAL THOMSON PUBLISHING COMPANY

PROFILES IN WORLD HISTORY
Significant Events and the People Who Shaped Them

Volume 2: Experimenting with Governments to Viking Invasion of Britain

Joyce Moss and George Wilson

Staff

Carol DeKane Nagel, *U•X•L Developmental Editor*
Julie L. Carnagie, *U•X•L Assistant Editor*
Thomas L. Romig, *U•X•L Publisher*

Shanna P. Heilveil, *Production Assistant*
Evi Seoud, *Assistant Production Manager*
Mary Beth Trimper, *Production Director*

Barbara A. Wallace, *Permissions Associate (Pictures)*

Mary Krzewinski, *Cover and Page Designer*
Cynthia Baldwin, *Art Director*

The Graphix Group, *Typesetting*

∞™ This book is printed on acid-free paper that meets the minimum requirements of American National Standard for Information Sciences—Permanence Paper for Printed Library Materials, ANSI Z39.48-1984.

ISBN 0-7876-0464-X (Set)
ISBN 0-7876-0465-8 (v. 1)   ISBN 0-7876-0469-0 (v. 5)
ISBN 0-7876-0466-6 (v. 2)   ISBN 0-7876-0470-4 (v. 6)
ISBN 0-7876-0467-4 (v. 3)   ISBN 0-7876-0471-2 (v. 7)
ISBN 0-7876-0468-2 (v. 4)   ISBN 0-7876-0472-0 (v. 8)

Printed in the United States of America

I(T)P™ U·X·L is an imprint of Gale Research,
an International Thomson Publishing Company.
ITP logo is a trademark under license.

Contents

Reader's Guide

Profiles in World History: Significant Events and the People Who Shaped Them presents the life stories of more than 175 individuals who have played key roles in world history. The biographies are clustered around 50 broad events, ranging from the Rise of Eastern Religions and Philosophies to the Expansion of World Powers, from Industrial Revolution to Winning African Independence. Each biography—complete in itself—contributes a singular outlook regarding an event; when taken as cluster, the biographies provide a variety of views and experiences, thereby offering a broad perspective on events that shaped the world.

Those whose stories are told in *Profiles in World History* meet one or more of the following criteria. The individuals:

- Represent viewpoints or groups involved in a major world event

- Directly affected the outcome of the event

- Exemplify a role played by common citizens in that event

Format

Profiles in World History volumes are arranged by chapter. Each chapter focuses on one particular event and opens with an overview and detailed time line of the event that places it in historical context. Following are biographical profiles of two to five diverse individuals who played active roles in the event.

Each biographical profile is divided into four sections:

- **Personal Background** provides details that predate and anticipate the individual's involvement in the event

- **Participation** describes the role played by the individual in the event and its impact on his or her life

- **Aftermath** discusses effects of the individual's actions and subsequent relevant events in the person's life

- **For More Information** provides sources for further reading on the individual

Additionally, sidebars containing interesting details about the events and individuals profiled are interspersed throughout the text.

Additional Features

Portraits, illustrations, and maps as well as excerpts from primary source materials are included in *Profiles in World History* to help bring history to life. Sources of all quoted material are cited parenthetically within the text, and complete bibliographic information is listed at the end of each biography. A full bibliography of scholarly sources consulted in preparing each volume appears in each book's back matter.

Cross references are made in the entries, directing readers to other entries within the volume that are connected in some way to the person under scrutiny. Additionally, each volume ends with a subject index, while Volume 8 concludes with a cumulative subject index, providing easy access to the people and events mentioned throughout *Profiles in World History.*

Comments and Suggestions

We welcome your comments on this work as well as your suggestions for individuals to be featured in future editions of *Profiles in World History.* Please write: Editors, *Profiles in World History,* U·X·L, 835 Penobscot Bldg., Detroit, Michigan 48226-4094; fax to 313-961-6348; or call toll-free: 1-800-877-4253.

Acknowledgments

The editors would like to thank the many people involved in the preparation of *Profiles in World History*.

For guidance in the choice of events and personalities, we are grateful to Ross Dunn, Professor of History at the University of California at San Diego, and David Smith, Professor of History at California Polytechnic University at Pomona. We're thankful to Professor Smith for his careful review of the entire series and his guidance toward key sources of information about personalities and events.

We deeply appreciate the writers who compiled data and contributed to the biographies: Diane Ahrens, Bill Boll, Quesiyah Ali Chavez, Charity-Jean Conklin, Mario Cutajar, Craig Hinkel, Hillary Manning, Lawrence Orr, Phillip T. Slattery, Colin Wells, and Susan Yun. We'd especially like to thank Jamie Mohn and Cheryl Steets for their careful attention to the manuscript.

Thanks also to the copy editors and proofreaders, Sonia Benson, Barbara C. Bigelow, Betz Des Chenes, Robert Griffin, Rob Nagel, and Paulette Petrimoulx, for their careful attention to style and detail. Special thanks to Margaret M. Johnson, Judith Kass, and John F. Petruccione for researching the illustrations and maps.

And, finally, thanks to Carol Nagel of U·X·L for overseeing the production of the series.

Picture Credits

The photographs and illustrations appearing in *Profiles in World History: Significant Events and the People Who Shaped Them,* Volume 2: *Experimenting with Governments to Viking Invasion of Britain* were received from the following sources:

On the cover: **The Granger Collection:** Julian the Apostate, Cleopatra, Muhammad.

Aga Khan Trust for Culture: p. 177; **The Bettmann Archive:** pp. 2, 8, 19, 27, 38, 50, 52, 62, 71, 73, 126, 130, 143, 165, 182, 187, 213; **The Granger Collection:** pp. 7, 12, 25, 40, 45, 46, 59, 77, 85, 97, 103, 115, 129, 137, 188, 195, 209; **Library of Congress:** pp. 69, 119, 141; **The Library, The Institute of Ismaili Studies, London:** p. 171; **Photo: Hirmer:** p. 153; **Snark International, Paris:** p. 17.

Experimenting with Governments

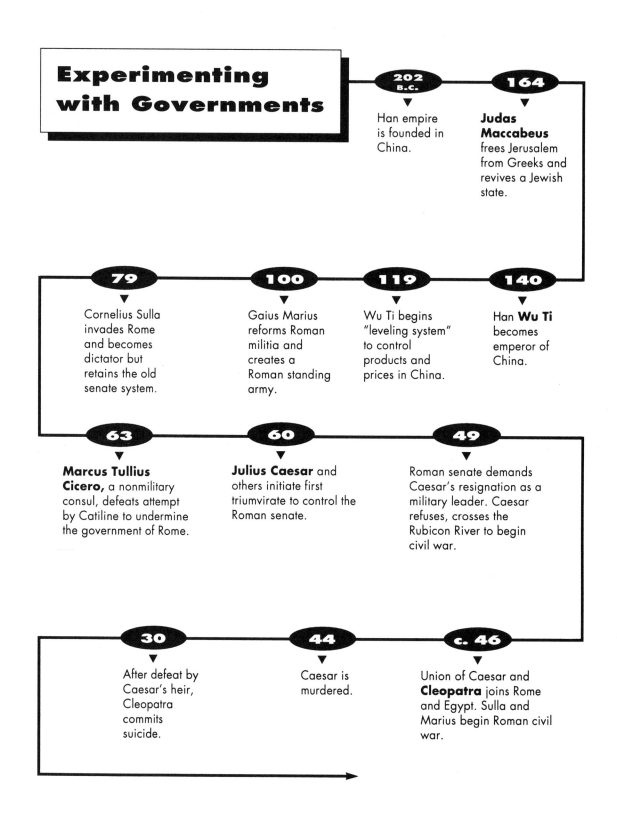

202 B.C. ▼ Han empire is founded in China.

164 ▼ **Judas Maccabeus** frees Jerusalem from Greeks and revives a Jewish state.

79 ▼ Cornelius Sulla invades Rome and becomes dictator but retains the old senate system.

100 ▼ Gaius Marius reforms Roman militia and creates a Roman standing army.

119 ▼ Wu Ti begins "leveling system" to control products and prices in China.

140 ▼ Han **Wu Ti** becomes emperor of China.

63 ▼ **Marcus Tullius Cicero,** a nonmilitary consul, defeats attempt by Catiline to undermine the government of Rome.

60 ▼ **Julius Caesar** and others initiate first triumvirate to control the Roman senate.

49 ▼ Roman senate demands Caesar's resignation as a military leader. Caesar refuses, crosses the Rubicon River to begin civil war.

30 ▼ After defeat by Caesar's heir, Cleopatra commits suicide.

44 ▼ Caesar is murdered.

c. 46 ▼ Union of Caesar and **Cleopatra** joins Rome and Egypt. Sulla and Marius begin Roman civil war.

EXPERIMENTING WITH GOVERNMENTS

Following the death of Alexander the Great in 323 B.C., his vast empire, which stretched east from Greece to the Himalayas of India, was divided. The Seleucid family of Greece became rulers of Syria and extended their empire along the coast toward Egypt. Their government was a dictatorship, as were most of the early empires. The Seleucids so closely controlled the lives of their citizens that the citizens were not allowed to practice their own religions. One group, the Hebrews, objected to this policy. **Judas Maccabeus,** a Hebrew from Jerusalem, led a rebellion against the Seleucids that finally established a religious civil government (a theocracy) in Jerusalem, although the Hebrews did not claim it to be so. It was the beginning of a period of experimentation with forms of government.

Two distant empires also were caught up in the spirit of change during the second and first centuries B.C. Rome and China, both with long-standing forms of government, had grown old, their people complacent. Revitalization of government seemed to be needed in both regions.

In its earliest days, Rome was ruled by a series of kings, as were the surrounding Etruscan city-states. In 509 B.C. Roman citizens overthrew a tyrannical king and replaced him with a repub-

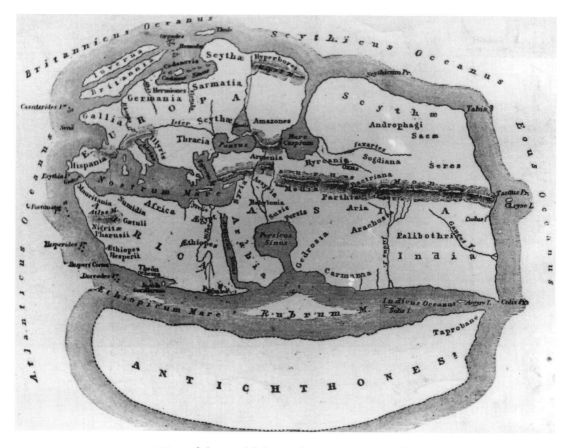

▲ Map of the world drawn by Pompomius Mela, a Latin geographer who lived during the first century A.D.

lican form of government. At first, while Rome was small, this government was nearly a true republic. Everyone, at least everyone who was male and owned land, could participate in government. But as some grew more wealthy and acquired more land, this upper class rose to have greater influence. A senate, or ruling body, of these prominent citizens was formed apart from the public assemblies and came to take great responsibilities, electing joint presidents called consuls and appointing judges, and, as Rome expanded its territory, provincial governors. Rules of government were established: an elected official could only occupy an office for a single year; the senate could appoint a dictator in times of emergency; a land-owning man must be thirty-five years old in order to run for office. Assemblies of the common people still existed and spoke to the senate through tribunes, elected officials who had the unpleasant task of opening their home doors at any hour to hear the complaints of people of all levels of wealth.

Although Rome prospered and expanded under this system, the government gradually changed. By the first century B.C., the senate had broken down into several cliques, each with its own agenda and each pushing its own candidate for consul. The divisions made for a corrupt and inept senate. Real power began to fall to the generals, who were called on frequently to lead wars to expand or maintain the empire and who, when chosen by whichever was the dominant segment of the senate, often became local dictators as the law prescribed.

Three major civil wars among powerful generals took place over a one-hundred-year period. Some of the generals claimed to be concerned with maintaining the republican structure and opposed those who would become dictators. In reality, the struggles were among powerful leaders who wanted to dictate the future of Rome. The first took place in 88 B.C. between Gaius Marius and Cornelius Sulla, with Sulla winning victory and establishing a short-lived dictatorship. Then Pompey the Great (Gnaeus Pompeius) and **Julius Caesar,** the former a victorious general in Italy, Spain, and Africa and the latter a ruler over Gaul (modern-day France) and England, conspired to control Rome.

For four years, while the old senate and assembly structure stood by helplessly, Caesar fought to become dictator of the empire. He sought to make the dictatorship permanent and to expand it, with the help of Egyptian queen **Cleopatra,** to include Egypt. After his death, the old republic almost revived, while Mark Antony, a prominent soldier and long-time friend to Caesar, and Caesar's adopted son Octavian (later Augustus Caesar) conspired to divide the vast realm. The end of this partnership resulted in a third civil war, from which Octavian emerged as emperor. The worn-out republic had been replaced by a dictatorship at last. Through much of this time, a real champion of the republic was working to keep the republican style of government alive. **Marcus Tullius Cicero,** though not a gov-

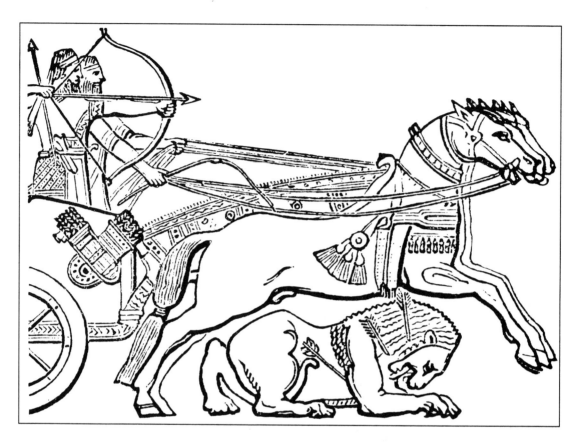

▲ A war chariot in the time of the pharaohs. Although the Ptolemy pharoahs—including Cleopatra—claimed to be descended from Egyptian gods, they were in fact Greek or Macedonian.

ernment official, defended the republic in court and wrote books about it that have influenced governments to this day.

Far off in China, the government had for thousands of years been run by family dynasties in which one individual who was supposedly chosen by God would serve as supreme ruler. For much longer than the Roman republic stood, Chinese rulers had passed the rule from one family member to another. Periodically, these families would lose interest in government duties or become too distant from and demanding of the people. Then that family would be overthrown and replaced by a new family dynasty. Thus the Chinese empire underwent periodic renewal. About 202 B.C., as the Roman republic began to decline, the existing dynasty of China gave way to a new family under the name of Han. But the initial surge of regroupment and prosperity begun by the middle of the second century B.C. gave way to apathy and tyranny. This time, however, a new Han emperor, **Wu Ti** (also spelled Wudi), came to the rescue.

Leaning heavily on the Confucian doctrine that taught the importance of everyone knowing his or her own place and playing that role for the good of the whole society, Wu Ti began vast reforms in Chinese government. Civil service jobs, formerly open only to the privileged class, were opened to appointment by examination (although the examination was merely a test of knowledge of Confucianism). Seeing the danger of a system that favored a few large landowners, Wu Ti initiated land reforms and systems for controlling prices and keeping them stable in times of both famine and prosperity. His reorganization was so successful that the government was able to support a revival of the arts and learning.

At the same time, Wu Ti, known as the Warrior Emperor, was able to devote his attention to expanding China both by trade and by territorial conquest. Although these changes did not inspire future emperors to reform, it had a lasting effect on the people of China. The revived Han dynasty would last for another three hundred years, and Confucianism would continue to influence Chinese life in the centuries following. But never after the Han dynasty expired would another dynasty arise to have such influence over China for such a long period of time.

Judas Maccabeus

?-160 B.C.

Personal Background

The family of Mattathias. Judas (or Judah) was the third of five sons of Mattathias, a high-ranking religious leader of the long-respected Hasmon family. Under the firm guidance of his father, the large and strong Judas developed an ability to fight as well as a tenderness and concern for other people and a very serious commitment to his religion. Very little record of Judas exists until his father decided to resist the Seleucids, Greeks who since Alexander the Great had ruled along the Mediterranean coast from southern Turkey through Syria and southward through Persia. The territory included Judea, which sat between Syria in the north and Egypt in the south and fell under the control of the Seleucids in 198 B.C.

Mattathias. Jewish, Greek, and Roman records tell of Mattathias, a patriarch of the Jews and a highly respected and deeply religious man who lived in the time of the Seleucid king Antiochus IV. Antiochus had his eye on reuniting Egypt with his own kingdom, which already had extended its rule to the small nation of Judea. Mostly inhabited by Jews, this nation and its capital city, Jerusalem, had been brutally treated by Antiochus ever since he decided that all his provinces be hellenized, or forced to adopt Greek ways.

Antiochus used a number of tactics to try to hellenize the Jews. He built a fort in Jerusalem called Acra, a citadel that housed

▲ **Judas Maccabeus**

Event: Winning religious and political independence for Judea.

Role: Judas Maccabeus assumed the leadership of a guerrilla group of religious Jews fighting for the right to independence in Judea. Eventually raising an army of ten thousand, Judas succeeded in winning religious independence for the Jews. He returned to Jerusalem as a leader of his people and restored the holiest of Jewish worship sites.

▲ **Relief sculpture from the Arch of Titus showing Romans pillaging the Temple of Jerusalem in** A.D. **70.**

Seleucid soldiers and provided shelter for hellenized Jews. He enthusiastically attacked the Jews and destroyed their articles of worship. He outlawed Judaism. Legend speaks of the tortures suffered by the Jewish elder Eleazar and seven younger men, brothers, all of whom preferred death to conversion. Frustrated in his attempt to use them as models to inspire the rest of the community to adopt Greek practices, Antiochus marched into Jerusalem and raided the temple, the Jews' most precious center of worship. He declared all symbols of Jewish worship be destroyed or given over to the worship of the Greek gods. To enforce this decree, in 167 B.C a Syrian-Greek army entered Jerusalem, seized the Jewish temple, and converted it to a temple of Zeus.

Antiochus's forces affirmed the destruction of Jewish practices by defiling the temple in the most egregious ways possible. Jews, believing that pigs were impure, had been forbidden in their religion to eat or sacrifice these animals. Antiochus, therefore, ruled that pigs should be sacrificed to the god Zeus upon the temple's great altar.

When Mattathias saw the temple defiled, he could no longer stand to live in Jerusalem. He moved a few miles away to Modin. With him went his five grown sons: Simon, Judas, Johanan, Eleazar, and Jonathan. They had only been in Modin a short time when agents of Antiochus arrived to force Greek religion on this town. Some Jews fled into the mountains to avoid this persecution, for they had little means of resistance. In fact, their own religion prevented total resistance—on the seventh day of each week, known as the Sabbath, devout Jews were not permitted to fight or even erect stone barriers to close the caves in which they were hiding to protect themselves. A few Jews, meanwhile, felt it wiser to adopt Greek beliefs and forsake their religion, or at least pretend to do so. Mattathias and his faithful sons took neither of these paths.

The traditional Jews, those who refused to stray from their own beliefs, had erected an altar at Modin for the worship of their own God. The Seleucids, not surprisingly, declared it an altar to Zeus and ordered the people of Modin to use it to sacrifice to the Greek god. One Jew did as commanded and sacrificed a pig on the altar. More than old Mattathias could stand, in a rage, he killed the heretic, fell on the Seleucid soldiers, and, with the aid of his sons and the other villagers, slew them all.

Mattathias knew it was necessary to flee to save his life. Bringing along the rest of the villagers, he and his sons took refuge in the nearby mountains of Gophna. The Seleucids would hunt them, as they did the other Jewish refugees, taking advantage of the Jewish Sabbath restrictions to destroy them. This was, however, a war for survival for Judaism and of the Jews. Mattathias, a high priest, declared that life was worthless without freedom of Jewish worship and that it was necessary to put aside the law long enough to fight the Seleucids. He and his sons called on all the most devout Jews to join them in resistance.

At first there were only about two hundred rebels who joined with the father and brothers—not enough to wage a full-scale war with the Seleucid army. So, Mattathias led his sons and followers in quick, covert guerrilla attacks on small groups of

Seleucids. The Jewish forces harassed the Seleucids for nearly a year, until Mattathias became ill and died.

Urged by their dying father, the sons carried on the battle. They all agreed that Simon would become the counselor for the group. Judas, the greatest warrior and most powerful to the lot, would lead the Jewish rebels in war. Somewhere along the way Judas received the surname Maccabeus. There is no record of the reason for his adopting this new name, which appropriately, may have its roots in the Aramaic word *makava,* meaning "hammer." Named after their leader, the rebels in the new Jewish resistance movement became known as the Maccabees.

Participation: Winning Religious and Political Independence

Guerrilla war. Judas proved a great leader in the guerrilla war started by his father. His forces attacked and destroyed places established for the worship of Greek gods while avoiding a direct conflict with the much larger Seleucid army. Finding him irksome, the Seleucids sent increasingly larger forces to defeat him.

In one larger battle, Judas fought and killed the Seleucid commander Apollonius. Judas took the dead officer's sword and carried it always as a symbol of ultimate victory for the Jews. As the guerrilla attacks and the confrontations with Seleucid soldiers grew, so did the loyalty of Judas' soldiers—and their numbers. Eventually, Judas would command an army of ten thousand soldiers.

Beth-horon. As Judas was building his army, so to were the Seleucids, and they attacked with sizable numbers in various places in Judea. Judas, now leading an army of about one thousand, prepared to face a force of about four thousand Seleucids under the direction of a general Seron that recently arrived at a town called Beth-horon, situated in a mountain pass in present-day Jordan, about eleven miles northwest of Jerusalem. Seron's soldiers began climbing the Beth-horon pass to Jerusalem, not suspecting that they were about to be ambushed on three sides by the Maccabees. Judas, his intelligence network having fore-warned him, had planned carefully. When the first unit of Seleucids reached the top of the pass, the Maccabees rushed at the enemy within the close confines of the pass—one unit attacked from the top, the other two from either side. The Seleucids were thoroughly defeated and forced to retreat. It was a major victory for Judas.

Ermannus. Again the two armies fought, this time at Ermannus, about four miles northwest of Jerusalem. Antiochus was off in Egypt and had given temporary rule to Lysius, the guardian of his son, Antiochus V. Lysius had gathered an army of twenty thousand, much larger than what Judas could raise (six thousand) and placed them under Seleucid generals Gorgias and Nicanor. Despite the numbers, Judas' superior leadership resulted in complete victory for the Jewish army. The stage was set for Judas' greatest confrontation with the Seleucid leaders.

Defending Jerusalem. In 165 B.C. Lysius once more returned to Judea with a massive army prepared to attack Jerusalem. Estimates place his troops at twenty thousand or more, while Judas had by now raised his forces to ten thousand. Lysius, however, did not choose to fight on Judas's terms. Instead his army marched around Jerusalem and prepared to enter the city through weaker enemy strongholds in the south. Judas gathered his army and confronted the Seleucids at a place called Beth-Zur, about twenty miles south southwest of Jerusalem (near present-day Hebron, Jordan). Once more, superior generalship won a victory for the Jews. Some historians believe that the loss of this battle prompted Lysius to agree to a Jewish return to Jerusalem. Whether that is true or not, the path was clear for the Jewish army to return to Jerusalem.

Restoring the temple. The first task of the pious Jews who had followed Judas was to reconstruct the temple. Rubbish was removed. New gold and silver articles of worship were brought in. The altar, defiled with sacrifices to Zeus, needed to be rebuilt completely. But because the old altar had been in the temple so long and no one wanted to discard it, it was dismantled stone by stone and stored in the garden near the temple. The Jews were

▲ French woodcut dating to 1514 depicting Judas Maccabeus and his four brothers in battle.

willing to wait until an ancient prophet told them what action to take. A new altar was built. All was in readiness.

On December 6, 164 B.C., the faithful gathered at the temple for the Feast of Dedication. For the first time in three years, a morning sacrifice was made in the restored temple. Judas decided that this celebration should be held each year in memory of the hard-fought battles through which the Jews of Judea renewed their religious freedom. This celebration continues today. The Feast of Dedication, better known as Hanukkah, still lasts for eight days, just as it did in 164 B.C.

In that same year, Judas began to consolidate the area around Jerusalem and make it safe for Jews. He sent his brother

Simon with three thousand soldiers to drive the hellenized Jews from Galilee (in modern-day northern Israel), and Jonathan undertook to control a rising threat from the Arabs in the south and east. His efforts took him to the coast of the Mediterranean Sea. A year earlier, Judas himself invaded a mostly non-Jewish settlement called Marpha, killing all the unbelieving men and taking the women and children as slaves.

Aftermath

Political freedom. The Jews, with Judas leading them, had secured religious freedom from the Greeks. But until political freedom was gained, however, the people of Jerusalem would always be threatened by the Seleucids. After Antiochus IV died in 164 B.C., he was officially replaced by his ten-year-old son Antiochus V. The boy's safety and upbringing had been transferred from the hands of Lysias to those of another Seleucid general, Philip. The ensuing tug-of-war for Seleucid control between Philip and Lysius would benefit the Jews.

The end of Lysius. In 163 B.C. Lysius, now claiming full control of Syria, organized a massive attack on Jerusalem, complete with fearsome elephants, the tanks of early warfare. The army entered Jerusalem and appeared about to put down all the Jewish resistance. Fortunately for the Jews, however, word reached Lysius that Philip was about to take control of the throne. Lysius rushed home to defend his claim.

> ## Judas Counsels His Troops Before the Battle of Emmaus
>
> "Do not be afraid of their great numbers or panic when they charge. Remember how our fathers were saved at the Red Sea, when Pharaoh and his army were pursuing them. Let us cry now to Heaven to favor our cause, to remember the covenant made with our fathers, and to crush this army before us today" (Judas in First Maccabees 4:8-11).

The timing was fortunate for the Jews, but the rush home was of little use to Lysius. By 162 B.C. both the young Antiochus and Lysius had been overthrown by Antiochus's cousin, Demetrius I Soter, and had been put to death. Still, the threat to the Jews remained. Demetrius appointed a foe of certain Jews, Alcimus, to be high priest of Jerusalem. One of Alcimus's first acts was to order the killing of sixty Jews. Judas asked the Syrian's arch enemy, Rome, for help. Very little came, and in 160 Judas found his reduced forces in pitched battle with the Seleucids once more—this time at a spot called Elasa. Twenty-two thousand Seleucids fought a small force of three thousand Maccabees (after winning religious freedom, the Maccabees forces dwindled), which shrank to eight hundred once the powerful enemy was spotted. In the battle Judas was killed and his soldiers defeated. Demetrius, however, proved not at all interested in religion, and so the Jews were allowed to maintain the freedom of worship that had been restored to them by Maccabeus.

Jonathan. A year after Judas' death, his brother Jonathan took up the cause and rallied the Jewish people into a new drive for political independence. He proved to be a skillful general in his own right, attacking the Seleucid army and driving it out of the region. Jonathan also proved to be a fine politician who could negotiate with the Seleucid leaders. Falling into a power struggle of their own, different Seleucids began to compete for Jonathan's (and Judea's) support. He was busy negotiating with them when he was killed by the Seleucid general Tryphon.

Simon. Once more Seleucia threatened. The tyrannical general Tryphon gathered a strong army and headed to Judea, planning to destroy the nation completely. Simon, another brother of Judas, now came to the fore and, with his careful thought and strong speaking skills, became leader of the Jews. Simon, however, understood better than his brothers the weak hold of the king of Seleucia. He petitioned Demetrius to win favors for Judea. His arguments and pleas won what war and diplomacy by Judas and Jonathan had not gained. In 142 B.C. Simon became the political

Judas Maccabeus, A Military Genius

**Battle
Enemy Leader
Number of Jews
Number of Greeks**

Gophna area
Appollonius
800
2,000

Beth-horon
Seron
1,000
4,000

Emmaus
Gorgias and Nicanor
6,000
20,000

Beth-Zur
Lysius
10,000
20,000+

The great numerical odds illustrate the greatness of Judas's military skill.

head and high priest of a land devoted to preserving the Jewish tradition. The next year, Simon's army drove the hellenized people from the citadel of Acra, and the bondage of the Jews was for the moment completely cast aside.

For More Information

Goldstein, Jonathan A., translator. *First Maccabees*. Garden City, New York: Doubleday, 1981.

Hirsh, Marilyn. *The Hanukkah Story*. New York: Bonim, 1974.

Pearlman, Moshe. *The Maccabees*. New York: Macmillan, 1973.

Wu Ti

156-87 B.C.

Personal Background

The Han dynasty. According to Chinese tradition, the founder of a dynasty was chosen by Heaven for his wisdom and service. Over the years, the successors of this founding father, it was believed, would grow further and further from service to the people and favor with Heaven. Eventually, a corrupt and evil member of the family would ascend to the throne and completely lose favor with Heaven. That person would be ousted and replaced by a new emperor more favorable to the deity. A new "dynasty" would then begin the cycle all over again. This in fact happened every few hundred years throughout the history of China.

In 202 B.C. a weak and dishonest Chinese emperor was overthrown and replaced by Kao Tsu (also spelled Gaozu) of the Han region. From his palace at Luoyang, the new emperor initiated a dynasty that would last for four hundred years, the Han. In 140 B.C. Liu Ch'i (or Liu Zhe) became the sixth emperor of the Han dynasty. He was sixteen years old when he took the throne under the name Wu Ti (also spelled Wudi). Later historians called him Han Wu Ti because there were other emperors named Wu Ti.

After the first Han emperor, the rulers of the Han dynasty championed literature and knowledge. The old order in China had once been set down in six historical texts, which had been destroyed by various rulers over the years. Revered philosopher

▲ **Wu Ti (center) visiting a renowned scholar to seek his opinion.**

Event: Creating a "leveling" system.

Role: During his reign as ruler of China, Wu Ti developed a program called *p'ing chun,* or leveling, in order to control prices, insure that the whole country was adequately supplied with produce, and raise money for the national treasury.

and teacher Confucius had recreated five of these books in the sixth and fifth centuries B.C. Under the Hans these texts were again brought forth and became guides for government. Moreover, government workers were accepted by an examination testing their knowledge of the Five Classics of Confucius.

In this climate that fostered learning, Wu Ti grew to become a well-educated man with a fondness for literature. More than the Han emperors who had preceded him, he enjoyed the company of scholars, who were often critics of the autocracy. But he was also ambitious and ruthless, and he had a violent temper that sometimes led him to commit rash acts that he would later regret. Wu Ti was distrustful as well, refusing to allow his high government officials any authority. Nevertheless, his accomplishments made him the greatest of the Han rulers.

Wu Ti's Magic and Science

Wu Ti, like other Han emperors before him, leaned heavily on sacrifice and magical religious rites and spent much of his time trying to win spiritual beings to his side. Magic and science, however, were very closely combined in his day. Indeed, Wu Ti's magicians made important observations in chemistry, magnetism, and the use of herbs in medicine. It was about the time of Wu Ti's reign that the greatest Chinese book of medicine was compiled, *Huang Di Nei Jing* ("The Yellow Emperor's Compendium of Corporeal Healing"). This book is still used in Chinese medicine. It contains the first detailed explanation of acupuncture.

Nomads. The overriding concern during Wu Ti's reign was the Hsiung-nu (also spelled Xiongnu), Turkic-speaking nomads who roamed the deserts and plains north of the Great Wall of China. The Great Wall was an earthen defensive wall averaging twenty-five feet high and twenty feet thick that stretched across fifteen hundred miles of north China, built in the third century B.C. to keep out northern marauders. The Hsiung-nu were continually raiding the border regions of China and had posed a constant threat for decades. Although Wu Ti would send ambassadors to nations as far distant as Bactria (in southwest Asia) asking for help in controlling the Hsiung-nu, he would never completely defeat them. The nomads would continue to threaten China for several centuries. In the fifth century A.D., a westward migrating Hsiung-nu horde would come to be known as the Huns.

Wu Ti's own ambition to acquire more territory, along with constant battles with the Hsiung-nu, earned him the nickname "Warrior Emperor." All of his ambitions, however, were not to be

▲ **Desert nomads; the overriding concern during Wu Ti's reign was the continued raiding by nomads who roamed the deserts and plains north of the Great Wall of China.**

achieved in battle. His quest to find allies to fight the Huns led him to discover the rich crops of Bactria. He established a thriving trade with that nation and other areas of Asia and Europe. As part of this expansion of trade, his armies conquered much of the land south of China, extending even into present-day Korea. Wu Ti established a trading center at Canton, now in southern China. Thus while Roman legions were expanding control in Europe and the Middle East, Wu Ti was building his own vast empire in Asia.

Feudalism. Another threat to Chinese unity was feudalism, a long-standing system of land ownership in which a few powerful nobles owned large tracts of land that were worked by serfs or slaves. The Han family had long struggled to reduce the power of these nobles. Wu Ti took up the struggle. In 127 B.C. he issued a decree requiring a nobleman's lands to be divided equally among his children upon his death. As a result, feudal estates were broken up within a few generations. Wu Ti began to create a new society by making nobles of "new men" such as merchants, government officials, and scholars. These new nobles, he figured, would be easier to manage than the old. Always poor because of his constant war activities, he even sold titles of nobility to enrich the state treasury.

Participation: Creating a Leveling System

New profiteers. The expansion of the nobility was not altogether successful. New wealthy nobles from among the merchants took advantage of the change to become tycoons who recruited gangs to terrorize the countryside. Salt and iron magnates became especially wealthy and independent. Much of China lacked salt, and iron was replacing bronze as the primary metal for tools and weapons. A few rich men made monopolies of these industries, buying raw materials when they were cheap, storing them until shortages appeared, and then selling at great profits. Their increasing accumulations of wealth lessened the funds available for government.

Wu Ti took several actions to curb wild buying and hoarding and to bring more money into the treasury. In 120 B.C. he put the government in control of the salt, iron, and alcoholic beverage industries. The following year, he imposed a series of new taxes. All merchants were to be charged 10 percent of every two thousand copper coins they collected. Craftsmen paid a lesser tax. Taxes were also imposed on carts and boats. Informers were encouraged to identify tax evaders, who would then face prison for a year and be forced to split his entire fortune with the informer. The new taxes produced the desired effect of increasing the treasury and discouraging personal savings; those with money spent it extravagantly. The law encouraging informers to expose fortunes was soon repealed.

The Conquests of Wu Ti

Wu Ti's army expanded Chinese influence eastward and southward. In 108 B.C. he invaded and conquered present-day northern Korea and opened the way for Chinese culture to reach Korea and Japan. Earlier he had conquered the kingdom of Nan Yue, or Nam Viet. By the time of his death he controlled almost all of present-day China, northern Korea, and Vietnam. He had also taken control of Ferghana, present-day Uzbekistan.

P'ing chun. But the problem of hoarding fortunes was still not completely solved. So Wu Ti and his economic adviser, Sang Hong-yang, devised a system for controlling prices. Introduced in 119 B.C., this system was called *p'ing chun (ping zhun)*, or leveling. Government agents were stationed around the countryside to buy up surplus products when prices fell. When shortages drove prices up, the government silos and barns were opened and government sales drove the prices down again.

In addition, Wu Ti instituted a distribution system. During the Han era, Chinese provinces had paid taxes to the central government in the form of a portion of the goods grown. Under *p'ing chun*, these taxes had to be paid in the type of produce most plentiful in a province. The government could then redistribute this produce to an area where it was scarce. For example, a rice-rich province would pay its tribute in the form of rice to be distributed to a province where rice was in short supply. This controlled speculating about the value of crops and price gouging during periods of shortage. A side benefit of the food program was employment. New roads, bridges, and canals needed for the exchanges of goods became part of massive public works projects.

Welfare? *Ping chun* appears to some historians to have been a form of welfare. Others felt that Wu Ti's major purpose was to raise funds more quickly. Buying at low prices and selling for more did bring considerable wealth to the state treasury. Apparently some of the Chinese saw this as a hidden tax, for Sang Hong-yang defended the program as a money maker:

> [The emperor] established the salt, iron, and liquor monopolies and the system for equitable [fair] marketing in order to raise more funds for the expenditures in the borders. Now our critics

The Adventures of a Wu Ti Ambassador

Soon after he took office, Wu Ti concocted a scheme to defeat the Hsiung-nu by enlisting the help of another northern tribe, the Yüeh-chih (also spelled Yuezhi), in present-day Manchuria and western China. There was one major obstacle: the Yüeh-chih had disappeared. Wu Ti sent an agent, Chang Ch'ien (or Zhang Qien), to find them and recruit them as allies. As soon as he was outside the Great Wall, Chang Ch'ien was captured by the enemy and held for ten years. Escaping, he continued his earlier mission and found the Yüeh-chih in present-day Afghanistan. They were no longer interested in their old homeland nor in fighting the Hsiung-nu. Eventually, Chang Ch'ien returned to China with tales of a land of superior horses, Ferghana, now Uzbekistan.

who desire that these measures be abolished would empty the treasuries and deplete the funds used for defense. (Sang Hong-yang in de Bary, p. 237)

Critics of reform. *P'ing chun* soon came under attack by some critics. Salt from the government salt monopoly became too expensive for most people to buy, and iron tools produced by government foundries were not only more expensive than privately made ones but were of poor quality. Confucian scholars, who longed for a return to the feudal past, also attacked the program for increasing the power of the emperor. The reforms did, however, bring price gouging under control—at least for a while.

Aftermath

A deadly mistake. Wu Ti's hasty and violent temper finally led him to commit an act he would later deeply regret. In 94 B.C. one of his favorite wives bore him a son. Ambitious for her son, this wife persuaded Wu Ti that his oldest son, whom he had willed to be the next emperor, was plotting against him. Without much investigation, the ruler ordered his eldest son put to death. Later, when further study revealed that his son had been innocent of the charge, Wu Ti ordered the accusing wife put to death. Nevertheless, on his death in 87 B.C., Wu Ti was succeeded by his seven-year-old son.

Beginning with this son, Wu Ti was succeeded by a series of weak rulers, and the authority of the central government faded. Alternating droughts and floods eventually forced prices to such high levels that the government was helpless to control them. In the year A.D. 9, an outsider, Wang Mang, overthrew the Han dynasty and set up a one-ruler-long dynasty before the Han family could restore their claim to rule.

For More Information

de Bary, Wing-tsit Chan, and Burton Watson. *Sources of Chinese Tradition.* New York: Columbia University Press, 1960.

Durant, Will. *Our Oriental Heritage.* New York: Simon and Schuster, 1954.

Fitzgerald, C. P. *China, A Short Cultural History*. New York: Frederick A. Praeger, 1954.

Gascoine, Bamber. *The Dynasties and Treasures of China*. New York: Viking, 1973.

Grousset, Rene. *The Rise and Splendour of the Chinese Empire*. Berkeley, California: University of California Press, 1953.

Latourette, Kenneth Scott. *A Short History of China*. New York: Macmillan, 1964.

Silverberg, Robert. *The Great Wall of China*. Philadelphia: Chilton Books, 1965.

Julius Caesar

100-44 B.C.

Personal Background

The Roman republic. Since the legendary founding of Rome in the ninth or eighth century , the city-state had been governed by a series of kings. In 509 B.C. the Romans overthrew their last king and established a republic (from the Latin expression meaning "people's thing"). The government of the new republic was divided into three parts: two men called consuls who acted together as president, a senate of established and wealthy noblemen, and people's assemblies. The senate, composed of former high government officials who had lifetime positions, controlled the government's money and determined its general policies. It also had, in times of emergency, the right to choose a dictator and give him absolute power to declare martial law, under which citizens could be executed without trial.

The people's assemblies, in which all citizens could vote, approved or rejected legislation and could declare war or make peace. The citizens could also elect tribunes, representatives who could veto senate legislation.

Consuls were the highest elected officials, corresponding roughly to American presidents—except that there were two in office at a time and they were elected for only a one-year term. Consuls had the power to call the senate into session and veto legislation, but could only act if they agreed with one another.

▲ **Julius Caesar**

Event: Reshaping Roman government.

Role: A prominent Roman politician, Julius Caesar expanded Roman rule in Europe through a series of military actions. After defeating his enemies in a civil war, he became undisputed leader of the Roman world. In this position, he initiated many reforms that endeared him to the peasant class and succeeded in replacing the aging republican government with a dictatorship.

When their terms ran out, consuls and other high officials were eligible for a one-year term as governor of a province, a territory conquered and governed by Rome, which served as the capital of the republic. Provincial governors could determine taxes and often grew rich by taking advantage of the local population. At the time Gaius Julius Caesar was born, the senate had split into small quarreling groups, and along with the republic, was rapidly becoming outdated.

To add to the troubles, other peoples of Italy who had been conquered by and allied to Rome were beginning to object that they were not allowed Roman citizenship. This disturbance would soon erupt into a rebellion known as the Italian War. When Caesar was still very young, a man who did not live in the city but was active in the people's party would lead the Roman army to defeat the other Italians. His courage, bravery, and knowledge of war would make this man, Gaius Marcius, an idol for the young Caesar.

Early life. The son of a government official, Julius Caesar came from an aristocratic family—one of the families that controlled the senate. There seems to have been no question of his destiny. Caesar's mother, Aurelia, planned for him to become a statesman. The way to political position was through the military, since Rome lived mostly on its conquests. So Aurelia saw to it that her son was well educated in politics and war. She hired a highly regarded tutor, Marcus Antonius, as a private teacher. Her selection later proved fortunate, for Antonius was from Gaul (present-day France), a place where Caesar would later spend much time and would build his reputation.

Caesar grew to be a tall, slender young man whose thin face suggested that he was always in deep thought. In contrast, his dark brown eyes seemed to shine with interest in those people and objects around him. He married twice before he was forty years old, and each marriage would deeply affect the direction of his career in politics.

Leaving Rome. When he was sixteen years old, his father died and, as was the tradition, Caesar became head of the household. While still a teenager, he married Cornelia, the daughter of an

▲ **The Forum under the caesars; as a curule aedile, Julius Caesar's duties included providing public entertainment.**

opponent of the dictator Cornelius Sulla, the most powerful man in Rome. This marriage made him an opponent of Sulla, a dangerous position in Rome. Caesar felt his prospects would be better if he left the city. He used his family's connections to gain a position on the staff of the governor of Rome's easternmost territory, Asia. After that experience, he began to study for a career in law.

To improve his skill as a speaker and lawyer, Caesar sailed to Rhodes, a Greek island near the coast of Turkey, to study under Apollonius Molon, the famous Greek teacher of debate. On the way to the island, Caesar was captured by pirates and held for ransom. After his release, he gathered some fighters and hunted down the pirates.

Return to Rome. When he completed his studies, Caesar joined the Roman army and fought in Asia Minor. Returning to Rome at age twenty-six, Caesar was elected as pontifex, a priest who presided over state religious ceremonies. He also practiced law and began to gain a reputation as a public speaker. His speaking caught the attention of Marcus Licinius Crassus, a wealthy and influential senator. Caesar soon became the senator's right-hand man.

A few years later, in 65 B.C., Caesar was elected to his first public office, a post called curule aedile. Perhaps this position could be compared to one in today's city building department or the parks and recreation department. Caesar's duties included providing public entertainment. With money borrowed from Crassus and others, Caesar staged lavish festivals that boosted his popularity with the masses.

With Crassus's help, Caesar began to climb the political ladder. He was elected pontifex maximus, or chief priest, of the Roman religion that called its chief god Jupiter. Soon afterward, he was elected praetor, which roughly corresponds to United States Supreme Court justice. The position of praetor raised him to rank among those who were eligible to be a provincial governor or to run for the senate. After his year of service, Caesar was assigned to be governor of a province in Spain.

In Spain. In Spain Caesar improved his military skills by leading troops against tribesmen who had not submitted to Roman rule. As governor, Caesar pushed through a number of reforms that included a law easing the burdens of debtors. His reform-mindedness gained him a popular following in Spain. A great benefit of being governor, however, was the privilege of collecting taxes. Through taxes and the booty from his military actions, he soon made so much money that he no longer had to depend on Crassus for funds.

Participation: Reshaping Roman Government

The First Triumvirate. In 62 B.C. the Roman general Pompey the Great (Gnaeus Pompeius) returned to Rome after a successful military campaign in Asia Minor. He found that he needed help in government to win approval of the treaties he had made and to secure the money he needed to pay his troops. Pompey saw Caesar as an ally who could help him get his legislation passed. Caesar, in turn, felt that the respect Pompey commanded would be useful to his own career. Two years later, Caesar returned from Spain and joined with Pompey and Crassus in a secret agreement to pool their wealth and work together to pass or oppose legislation. Their three-man union became known as the triumvirate, from the Latin term meaning "three men." To strengthen the alliance, Caesar gave Pompey his only daughter, Julia, for his wife.

Consul Caesar. The triumvirate's power was soon demonstrated when Caesar was elected consul for the year 59 B.C. During his year in office, Caesar introduced legislation that provided grants for Pompey's veterans and for Rome's urban poor as well. Wealthy members of the senate strongly opposed these measures, so Caesar took his bill to the people's assembly. Impressed by the triumvirate's show of unity and fearful of thugs recruited by Caesar, the assembly passed the bill. Caesar then shut down the senate by refusing to call it into session and overruling his co-consul when he tried to do so.

When the consul term expired, Caesar was eligible to be appointed a provincial governor. He secured the governorship of Cisalpine Gaul, a region comprising northern Italy and Illyricum (now Croatia). When the governor of the more northern province died, Caesar was awarded the governorship of Transalpine Gaul, now southern France.

The Gallic Wars. Soon after Caesar arrived in Gaul, trouble broke out in northern, "wild" Gaul beyond Roman territory. One entire tribe, the Helvetii, was trying to move from its home in present-day Switzerland to the Atlantic coast. The Romans believed that this tribe might upset Roman Gaul by an invasion or by driving other neighboring peoples from their own homelands.

The troubles in Gaul provided Caesar an opportunity to gain military glory and prestige. He moved his troops into northern Gaul, defeated the Helvetii near Lake Geneva, and halted their migration. In short order, he defeated other Gallic and German tribes. He even had his soldiers build a bridge across the Rhine River and raid German territory never before entered by Romans. By 55 B.C. he had completed his conquest of Gaul, except for local revolts that erupted from time to time over the next few years. Caesar capitalized on his successes by sending frequent reports to Rome. These brought him great popularity in the capital city.

In 55 and 54 B.C. Caesar crossed the English Channel with an army to invade the island of Britain. Although he defeated the island's Gallic people, he soon left after finding that Britain contained little wealth and much bad weather.

Decline of the triumvirate. In 56 B.C. Caesar met with Pompey and Crassus at Luca (now Lucca), in Cisalpine Gaul. The three sought to patch up growing differences among them. The meeting failed, and the triumvirate soon began to fall apart. Pompey drew away from Caesar after the death of Pompey's wife Julia in 54 B.C. The next year, Crassus died fighting in what is now Iran, and the following year, Publius Clodius, an aristocrat and powerful mob leader who had supported the triumvirate, was killed in a street fight.

The death of Clodius was felt in Gaul. Believing that Caesar would now have to return to Rome to regain his authority, Gauls began to revolt. Their troops initially defeated Caesar's army and forced a retreat. However, the Gallic leader, Vercingetorix, soon found himself surrounded by Caesar's men. Caesar fought off a much larger relief force, and Vercingetorix surrendered at Alesia, a town near modern Dijon, France.

Civil war. While Caesar was busy with the revolt in Gaul, his enemies among the Roman senators rallied to support Pompey. They demanded that Caesar disband his army and return to Rome as a private citizen. Knowing that he would be accused of abusing his power when he had crossed the Rhine River and when he had invaded Britain, Caesar tried unsuccessfully to negotiate with Pompey. In 49 B.C., instead of disbanding his army, he marched it across the Rubicon, the river separating Gaul and Italy, shouting, "Iacta alea est!" ("The die is cast!") Caesar was now at war with his former ally Pompey.

The two armies fought on several fronts. After seizing Rome and defeating Pompey's allies in Spain, Caesar made a reckless move. He underestimated Pompey's ability to organize resistance

▲ *Caesar Sailing the Thames,* a sixteenth-century woodcut depicting Julius Caesar's invasion of Britain.

in Greece. With too few men, Caesar landed on its coast and was defeated by Pompey's recruits. Caesar was chased into central Greece, where he reorganized and beat Pompey's army so badly that Pompey was forced to flee to Egypt.

Caesar and Cleopatra. In another show of boldness and recklessness, in 48 B.C. Caesar set out after Pompey with only three thousand men and ten ships. Upon arriving in Egypt, he learned that the boy-king Ptolemy XIV and his powerful court advisers had ordered Pompey murdered. Nevertheless, Caesar's small force occupied the royal palace. The king had recently thrown out his sister and co-ruler **Cleopatra VII** (see entry). She had raised an army of her own to try to regain the throne. Caesar demanded that the two again be co-rulers and repay the debts their father had run up with the Romans, money that was needed to pay the Roman troops. Hoping that Caesar would help her regain her throne, Cleopatra returned to the palace. (Legend has it that she arrived rolled up in a carpet to evade Ptolemy's troops.) Once she had arrived, Caesar and Cleopatra immediately began an amorous relationship.

Soon afterward, Ptolemy began a rebellion against the better-trained Romans. In the struggles, Ptolemy was killed, and Caesar then gained control of Egypt. Soon he encountered a new crisis. Pharnasus II of Pontus was threatening Roman territory in Asia Minor. Caesar easily defeated this opposition, afterward boasting, "Veni, vidi, vici!" ("I came, I saw, I conquered!").

Pompey's supporters continued to resist, though continually pursued by Caesar. He crushed the Pompeians in Africa, and the following year he fought his last battle with them, defeating the opposition in Spain. Caesar now had absolute power in the Roman republic. In fact, he had even once been elected dictator of Rome—for eleven days.

Aftermath

The senate and the dictator. The powerless senate now regularly renewed Caesar's consulship and eventually named him dictator for life. Caesar began dressing like the ancient kings and even had a throne installed in the senate building. It seemed that he might be preparing to establish a monarchy. However, realizing that many Romans still hoped for a strong republic, Caesar put off being crowned king or emperor.

Reforms. As absolute ruler, Caesar was able to make a number of reforms. He demanded laws making it easier for debtors to repay their creditors, he extended Roman citizenship to other Italians, and he introduced a new calendar. His Julian calendar was a great improvement over an earlier, inaccurate one and so became the foundation for the Gregorian calendar of today. Caesar also sent Romans to newly conquered territories, where they established communities and eased the spread of Roman culture.

In late 45 B.C., Caesar decided to organize a military expedition to conquer Parthia, a kingdom in the Middle East. Besides providing Rome with more riches and opening trade routes to China and India, such an expedition would allow Caesar to follow in the footsteps of a former great conqueror, Alexander the Great. The Romans were scheduled to leave on this journey on March 19, 44 B.C.

Meanwhile, Marcus Brutus and Gaius Cassius, two senators who were alarmed at Caesar's increasing powers, began to plot his death. On March 15, the Ides of March, when many of Caesar's supporters were away at a religious festival, Brutus and Cassius, along with several other plotters, pulled daggers from their togas and attacked Caesar at a senate meeting. Caesar died after receiving twenty-three wounds. He fell at the foot of a statue of Pompey.

Caesar's assassination failed to restore the republic. A long power struggle began, which Octavian, Caesar's adopted son and heir, finally won. Octavian would eventually establish a Roman empire.

For More Information

Barrow, R. H. *The Romans.* Hammondsworth, England: Penguin Books, 1968.

Bruns, Roger. *Julius Caesar.* New York: Chelsea House, 1987.

Dickinson, John. *Death of a Republic: Politics and Political Thought in Ancient Rome, 59-44 b.c.* New York: Macmillan, 1963.

Grant, Michael. *Caesar.* Chicago: Follett, 1974.

Weigall, Arthur. *The Life and Times of Cleopatra, Queen of Egypt.* New York: Putnam's, 1924.

Marcus Tullius Cicero

106-43 B.C.

Personal Background

Early life. For several hundred years, ownership of the land around Rome had been changing. At first, individual peasants owned and farmed small plots of land, but as more and more slaves were brought into the area and put to work on the land, the size of the farms around Rome gradually increased. By Cicero's time, most of the land was owned by a few men wealthy enough to buy the slaves needed for the work. Many of the wealthy landowners became horsemen and knights in the Roman legions. Called equestrians, some of these men had great hopes for gaining influence in Roman government. That government was, in the first century B.C., a declining republic that had grown corrupt over a span of four hundred years.

Marcus Tullius Cicero was born in Arpinum, now Arpino, about sixty miles southeast of Rome, the son of an equestrian and knight. His father was intent on having his son take an active interest in government and reaching a high position in Rome. When Cicero was a teenager, he was sent to Rome to absorb the city's culture and study under Crassus, a well-known orator, or master of public speaking and argument. Cicero learned Greek and studied Greek literature as part of his broad education; and he developed an interest in law. Lawsuits, at that time, were heard in the Forum, the meeting place of the Roman courts, by juries of

▲ **Marcus Tullius Cicero**

Event: Defending the Roman republic.

Role: Orator, statesman, and philosopher Marcus Tullius Cicero is said to have been able to speak "as no Roman ever spoke before or after." Cicero, in his speeches and writings, championed republican principles and constitutional government. His impact on political thought has endured to the present day.

▲ The remains of the Forum, the meeting place of the Roman courts; in Cicero's time, lawsuits were heard by juries of seventy-five or eighty men.

seventy-five or eighty men. The nature of these trials forced lawyers to become orators, relying on their public speaking ability for success. Cicero tried to learn oratory by memorizing, reading, and writing poetry. But that was not enough; as a young man, he became convinced that to be an orator he needed to have a knowledge of almost everything. He therefore studied philosophy in three different schools. Except for a short time spent in the Roman army led by Cornelius Sulla, Cicero was a student until he was twenty-six years old.

At that age, Cicero argued his first major case, successfully defending the accused murderer, and published the speech he had made in the man's defense. But Cicero, still not satisfied with his abilities, visited the Greek island of Rhodes, where Apollonius Molon (later the teacher of **Julius Caesar** [see entry]) helped him improve his oratorical skills.

Politician. Back in Rome after three years of study under Molon, Cicero again took up his work as a lawyer. He soon gained a following among equestrians, members of his father's class of knights who were landowners, professionals, and businessmen. He began handling their legal work. In 76 B.C., however, at the age of thirty, Cicero became eligible to run for office and was elected quaestor, or treasurer, of western Sicily. There was a shortage of grain in Rome, and Sicily was a grain-producing region. As quaestor, Cicero proved to be fair as well as efficient. He was able to supply Rome with grain without starving the Sicilians. He won cooperation from the grain-growers with his fairness, sense of justice, and approachability.

Slaves in Rome

The population of Rome in Cicero's time was greatly dependent on the bounty of frequent wars. Some of this bounty was in the form of slaves. These captured people made up as much as one-third of the population and performed most of the manual labor in Rome. Publishers had teams of slaves copy manuscripts by hand for sale in bookstores. The manuscript of the speech that Cicero delivered at his first major trial, and speeches of subsequent trials, were produced in this way.

Romans, at that time, were elected to office for a single year. After his year-long term expired, Cicero returned to practicing law in Rome. Five years later, the Sicilians wanted to prosecute a former governor for corruption in office. Cicero was invited to handle the case. Because he was planning to run again for public office, he saw this as an opportunity to increase his popularity. Cicero successfully prosecuted the ex-governor, Verres, denouncing his misdeeds while defending republican values. Although Verres was supported by powerful nobles and defended by an important man who would in the future become consul (a president) of Rome, Cicero won the case.

▲ An engraving from a painting by R. Cogghe of Romans selling Iberians as slaves.

While the trial was still in progress, he was elected curule aedile, or civil administrator of Rome. Among the aedile's responsibilities were the staging of games and entertainment and overseeing Rome's grain supply. Unlike Julius Caesar when he was in this position, Cicero spent modestly on entertainment. He also used his office to support acts of kindness, aiding debtors and victims of bandits and pirates. His popularity grew, especially among the equestrians, and he was elected praetor, a high-ranking judge.

At the same time that he was serving as praetor, war was beginning in the Roman territories to the east, in Asia Minor. In Rome a movement arose to name Pompey the Great (Gnaeus Pompeius), a hero in recent wars against rebellious slaves and pirates, supreme commander of Roman troops in this new war. Cicero supported this movement. He delivered a passionate speech to the senate calling Pompey an ideal commander, and

Pompey won the assignment. Cicero would remain a supporter of the great general until Pompey's death.

Participation: Defending the Roman Republic

Consul Cicero. After leaving the post of praetor, Cicero ran for and won election in 63 B.C. to the office of consul, one of the two presidents of Rome. This was the first in a series of actions supporting the republic that earned him his reputation as the "father of his country" and eventually much public praise. He was later honored by public thanksgivings dedicated to the gods.

Cicero and Rullus. Cicero took office in the midst of hard times. The war in Asia Minor had upset the economy, and food supplies were low. These conditions created a political climate favorable to radicals and, in fact, anyone who wanted to make changes. A tribune (a ruler elected from the people's assemblies) named Publius Servilius Rullus had been promoting a scheme to distribute land to veterans and the poor. A commission in charge of this scheme would have power to raise armies and acquire foreign territories. Fearing that such secondary armies would divide and threaten the republic, Cicero vigorously attacked the bill and finally defeated it.

Part of the record of Cicero's service as consul is lost, but he is known to have pushed two bills through the senate. One opposed bribery and the other restricted the rights of nobles to tour the provinces in order to secure bribes and payoffs.

Cicero and Catiline. Toward the end of his consulship, Cicero grew concerned with the activities of Lucius Sergius Catiline, a radical nobleman. Catiline had run unsuccessfully for consul a year before and was running again and calling for radical measures such as cancelling all debts. Cicero opposed his candidacy. After Catiline was defeated, rumors circulated that he was plotting a rebellion.

Cicero asked the senate to declare martial law, which would give him and his co-consul power to deal with the situation. The rebellion never came about, but later Catiline appeared at a senate

▲ Cicero speaking out against Catiline in the Roman senate, a detail from a mural by Cesare Maccari.

meeting. That gave Cicero an opportunity to speak against him and accuse him of plotting to overthrow the government. Cicero urged Catiline to leave Rome. The rebel responded by insulting the consul and sneering at his rural background. That night, however, Catiline left Rome and joined a band of rebels in the hills to the north.

A few weeks later, Cicero intercepted letters from four senators who supported Catiline. From these he learned that a new rebellion was going to take place on the Saturnalia, the Roman counterpart of Christmas, December 17. The rebels planned to murder senators and start fires throughout Rome.

Cicero called the senate into session on December 3 and read the letters aloud. He then ordered the four plotting senators jailed. Rejecting pleas for mercy from, among others, Julius Caesar, Cicero used his authority under martial law to have the men strangled. He had his co-consul then send troops out to deal with Catiline. However, the old rebel died in 62 B.C.

Cicero and Julius Caesar. At the end of his year as consul, Cicero became a leader in the senate. He was soon in conflict with Caesar, a popular army general. Caesar, Pompey, and Marcus Licinius Crassus, a wealthy senator, had decided to pool their wealth and form a triumvirate to dominate Roman politics. The three men invited Cicero to join them, but he refused. Caesar had just retired from a year as consul and planned to close down the senate in that year. Cicero was alarmed; he felt that Caesar was becoming too much of a dictator.

Caesar respected and feared Cicero's power of persuasion, so he responded by encouraging Publius Clodius, another nobleman, to take a position opposing the great speaker. Three years earlier, Cicero had prosecuted Clodius for defiling a religious ceremony. Clodius fell in with Caesar's triumvirate when one of them bribed the jury to acquit him. Later the three power-managers arranged for Clodius to be elected tribune, the people's representative in government.

As tribune backed by the big three of Roman politics, Clodius introduced a law calling for the exile of anyone who put Roman citizens to death without a trial. The law was aimed at Cicero, who, four years earlier, had ordered the execution of four rebellious senators. Fearing for his life, Cicero fled to southern Italy. On the recommendation of Clodius, he was then declared an outlaw and expelled from Italy. His property taken and his house burned, Cicero headed for Thessaloniki, Greece, to spend the most miserable year of his life.

Meanwhile, opposition to Clodius grew. It reached a climax when one of his hired thugs killed a friend of Pompey. The old general now led a fight to allow Cicero to return. Cicero was soon back in Rome.

Cicero then tried to have his property restored. In a senate speech, he claimed that the laws under which he had been exiled were unconstitutional. He told the senate he had been evicted by violence and scare tactics and that the sentence had been passed without a trial. The principles of fairness that Cicero defended as part of the Roman constitution are still found in American legal thought.

Although the senate voted to repay him for his losses, Clodius's thugs attacked the workers restoring Cicero's home. The two would remain enemies for life. In 52 B.C., when Clodius was killed in a street fight, Cicero acted as attorney for the murderer.

Writing about the republic. By 59 B.C., with the triumvirate controlling Roman politics and government, Cicero drifted out of public life and turned to writing. His most important work was *De republica* ("On the Republic"), six volumes of political philosophy. In these volumes, he analyzed three forms of government: monarchy, aristocracy, and democracy. He argued that each of these forms of government could become defective: a monarchy could fall into tyranny; an aristocracy could become an oligarchy (rule by a few); and democracy could revert to mob rule. The best form of government, he felt, was a combination of the three. His ideal was the Roman republic in the second century B.C., before the conquests, land reforms, and triumvirates.

As a companion to "On the Republic," Cicero began writing *De legibus* ("On the Laws"), a book he would never complete. In "On the Laws," he proposed that there was a higher natural law, which he described as "right reason in agreement with Nature" (Kirk, p. 108). In other words, he felt there were universal rules that were set down by God or derived from the nature of man. Cicero argued that citizens are under no obligation to obey an unjust ruler, especially one who violates the constitution or natural law. These principles of natural law and constitutionalism can be found today in the American Declaration of Independence as well.

Aftermath

Cilicia. Cicero was now separated from Roman government by a senate edict requiring all ex-consuls to serve as governors of foreign provinces. Cicero was assigned to Cilicia in Asia Minor. After the year of service, he returned to Rome to find a civil war underway.

Civil war. Caesar, who by now had distinguished himself as a powerful general who set his sights on becoming dictator of Rome, refused to obey a government edict to disband his army.

Instead, in 49 B.C. he led his army into civil war with Rome. Pompey opposed him, and Cicero sided with his old ally. When Caesar overran Italy with his troops, Cicero and Pompey fled to Greece. There Pompey died, and Cicero refused an offer to take command of Pompey's army. Though he was a man of virtue and a champion of the republic, he also was aware of the changing power structure. Seeing victory for Caesar, Cicero decided to return to Italy and make peace with the new Roman dictator. This move against his own principles would ultimately lead to his downfall.

Return to writing. After the war, Cicero returned to writing. He published a textbook on public speaking, *De oratore* ("On Oratory"), that would be used for the next two thousand years. Then he turned to philosophy. In the *Hortensius,* he argued that the life of a scholar was preferable to the traditional Roman goals: money-making, war, and politics. Four hundred years later, the book inspired the conversion of St. Augustine.

End of the republic. Caesar was murdered in 44 B.C., and Mark Antony, a prominent soldier and a lifelong supporter of Caesar, took charge in Rome. Later that year, Cicero spoke against Antony in a series of speeches known as the *Philippics.* The two were soon trading personal attacks.

The following year, Antony allied with Octavian, Caesar's adopted son (later Augustus Caesar), and Marcus Lepidus to form another triumvirate. The new team determined to destroy their opponents. They made a list of two thousand businessmen and three hundred senators marked for death. On Antony's insistence, Cicero's name was added to the list. Soldiers found Cicero at his home and ran him through with their swords.

For More Information

Dickinson, John. *Death of a Republic: Politics and Political Thought in Ancient Rome, 59-44 b.c.* New York: Macmillan, 1963. Source of opening quote, p. 35.

Kirk, Russell. *The Roots of American Order.* Washington, D.C.: Regnery Gateway, 1991.

Lacey, W. K. *Cicero and the End of the Roman Republic.* London: Hodder and Stoughton, 1978.

Langguth, A. J. *A Noise of War.* New York: Simon and Schuster, 1994.

Cleopatra VII

69-30 B.C.

Personal Background

The setting in Egypt. After the death of Alexander the Great of Macedon in 323 B.C., Ptolemy, one of his generals, seized control of Egypt, making himself pharaoh, or king. Thus began a dynasty of sixteen Ptolemys and seven Cleopatras. Although these pharaohs claimed to be descended from Egyptian gods, they were in fact Greek or Macedonian. Of these twenty-three rulers, only the last, Cleopatra VII, bothered to learn Egyptian, the language of most of their subjects. Alexandria, the capital city, had been constructed as a Greek city, but by the time of Cleopatra, it was beginning to show some Egyptian influence.

Like the rulers before them, the Ptolemy were absolute monarchs. Each owned all the land and much of the business and industry of Egypt. Though they intermarried among themselves, the Ptolemy frequently plotted against and assassinated other family members.

Egypt under the Ptolemaic dynasty was a very wealthy country. Farmers in the Nile delta produced great amounts of grain. Major trade routes passed through Egypt, and merchants from Alexandria carried out a thriving trade with Arabia and India. Since the Battle of Pydna in 169 B.C., in which the Romans defeated Macedon to become the strongest military power in the eastern Mediterranean area, Rome had taken an increasing inter-

▲ **Cleopatra VII**

Event: Undermining Roman rule.

Role: After winning a power struggle for control of Egypt with the aid of Julius Caesar, Cleopatra tried to combine Egypt and Rome into a united empire. After Caesar's death, she won Mark Antony to her cause and aided him in his losing struggle with Octavian for control of the Roman world.

est in Egypt, eager to share in its wealth. The Romans soon began interfering in Egyptian affairs. In what was at first an Egyptian issue, Ptolemy XIII, known as Ptolemy the Flute Player, was overthrown. He offered Rome a significant bribe, and Roman troops appeared to restore the pharaoh to power, thereby ensuring Roman influence in Egypt. By the time Cleopatra VII was born, Egypt had become nearly a Roman protectorate, or controlled province.

Cleopatra VII and the throne. Cleopatra was born into the royal Greek-Egyptian family in 69 B.C. She was the seventh of the Cleopatras, and the daughter of Ptolemy the Flute Player. As a child, she was educated as a future ruler of Egypt and learned several languages, including Egyptian. She grew to be an ambitious and ruthless young woman who hoped to restore Egypt to the great power it had been during the early years of the dynasty.

Cleopatra was about fifteen years old and her brother, Ptolemy XIV, was ten when their father died. His will called for his daughter and son to rule jointly. It also requested the Romans to be protectors of the kingdom. A copy of this will was filed in Alexandria, then Egypt's capital city, and another sent to Rome. The copy for Rome, however, was intercepted by the Roman general Pompey the Great (Gnaeus Pompeius).

Exile. Besides being very young, Ptolemy XIV turned out to be very easily influenced. After three years of joint rule, his advisers suggested that he oust his sister and rule alone. To this he agreed, and court attendants loyal to the king soon took control of the country. Cleopatra was forced to escape to Syria, where she raised an army and went to war against her brother to regain the throne.

Participation: Undermining Roman Rule

The Romans. Meanwhile Pompey had just been defeated in a Roman civil war by **Julius Caesar** (see entry) and fled to Egypt in

A bas-relief of Cleopatra VII from the Temple at Dendera.

48 B.C. Caesar, who now had absolute power in the Roman republic, pursued Pompey into Egypt. Upon arriving, however, he learned that Pompey had been murdered by Ptolemy's advisers. His enemy now dead, Caesar arrived in Egypt and occupied the royal palace at Alexandria, claiming to act as Egypt's "protector." Holding Ptolemy under house arrest, Caesar demanded that Egypt pay him the debt run up in the protection of Ptolemy the Flute Player.

Reclaiming the throne. With her military campaign an apparent failure, Cleopatra now plotted to win back her throne through Caesar. Arriving by sea off the coast near Alexandria, she slipped into the harbor in a small boat and then, according to legend, was smuggled into the palace past Ptolemy's guards, hidden inside a rolled-up carpet. By the next morning, she had won Caesar over to her cause.

Cleopatra and Caesar. Meanwhile, Ptolemy's faithful attendants were organizing resistance. The people of Alexandria were aroused, and forces began to lay siege to the palace. Caesar turned the palace into a fort, sent raiders to burn Egyptian ships, and seized the harbor to allow Roman reinforcements to enter Alexandria. Taking an active part in these military affairs, he was nearly killed by Egyptians before swimming to safety.

It was soon learned that reinforcements were on their way, and Ptolemy slipped out of the palace, only to be killed in a battle with pro-Roman forces. Although Roman forces overran Egypt, the dynastic tradition now made Cleopatra's young half-brother Ptolemy XV co-ruler. However, in actuality, Caesar and Cleopatra now controlled Egypt. The two had similar goals. She wanted to use her relationship with Caesar to make Egypt a partner in a vast Egypto-Roman empire, while he hoped to use their relationship to extend Roman rule over Egypt.

Caesar remained in Egypt with Cleopatra while his henchman Mark Antony ran affairs in Rome. Although the couple was never married (Caesar already had a wife in Rome), the native Egyptian priesthood seemed to recognize Caesar as Cleopatra's legitimate husband. She claimed he was the personification of the Egyptian god Amon. Thus a Greek and a Roman claimed to be authentic Egyptian rulers.

In 47 B.C. the queen of Egypt gave Caesar his first and only son. Later her enemies would raise questions as to whether Caesar was the father, but she named the son Caesarion, a Greek name for "Little Caesar."

Rome. Within a year, Caesar's position in Rome grew shaky. Followers of his old enemy Pompey were rallying. Riots and mutinies were common occurrences in Italy, and the king of Pontus was threatening Roman rule in Asia Minor. Caesar returned to Rome. Once he had restored order, he sent for Cleopatra. The queen of Egypt stayed in the house of the ruler of Rome.

Cleopatra was of a royal family and was resented by the republican-minded Romans, including former counsel **Marcus Tullius Cicero** (see entry). Nevertheless, Rome soon felt her influence. Alexandrian astronomers were called to design a new calendar for Rome. Egyptians came to Rome to build sets for the entertainment spectacles. Caesar had seen the canals and swamp drainage projects in Egypt and now planned similar large public works for Rome. He also planned to build large libraries in Rome like the one he had seen in Alexandria. Cleopatra's heritage as an absolute monarch may have influenced Caesar, or perhaps he wanted to pass Rome, as a kingdom, to his only son.

About 45 B.C. Ptolemy XV died. Cleopatra's enemies claimed she poisoned him. In the Ptolemaic tradition, Caesarion became King Ptolemy XVI.

Cleopatra and Antony. Caesar was assassinated in 44 B.C. by a group of Roman senators who disapproved of Caesar's increasing appetite for power. His will named his adopted son Octavian (later Augustus Caesar) as his heir. He had provided nothing for Cleopatra or Caesarion; it would have been a violation of Roman law to do so. Cleopatra and Caesarion left Rome. Soon afterward, Octavian, Mark Antony, and the military officer Marcus Lepidus, who together formed the Second Triumvirate, agreed to divide the Roman world among themselves.

Because the triumvirate included Octavian, Caesarion's rival as Caesar's heir, Cleopatra opposed it. She may even have aided

▲ **Cleopatra VII and Mark Antony cruising the Nile; at Tarsus, crowds had lined the shore to watch Cleopatra arrive.**

Marcus Brutus and Gaius Cassius, the men who led the plot to kill Caesar, in raising an army to fight the three new leaders.

In 42 B.C. Antony defeated the armies of Brutus and Cassius and then marched to Rome's eastern provinces to claim the authority of the triumvirate. The following year, he called Cleopatra to meet him at Tarsus in Asia Minor to answer charges that she had been aiding his two enemies. Caesarion was still too young to lead armies to overthrow Octavian. So Cleopatra duly left for Tarsus, hoping to win over Antony as she had Caesar.

Entertaining Antony. At Tarsus, crowds lined the shore to watch Cleopatra arrive aboard a barge with purple sails, silver oars, and a stern overlaid with gold. She invited Antony aboard and entertained him with great banquets complete with dancers, musicians, and golden dishes. The display of wealth helped win over Antony, who, although physically strong and a good military commander, was also a playboy. Antony, however, was also intelligent enough to realize that a union with the beautiful Egyptian queen would secure his claim on the eastern Mediterranean. He accepted her invitation to visit Egypt and, late in the year, sailed for Alexandria.

Again Cleopatra planned rich entertainment upon his arrival. Antony, like Caesar, took up residence with her. This time the union produced twins. One of the twins, Cleopatra Selene, would later become queen of Numidia, a Roman protectorate.

Trouble with Octavian. Soon there were again problems in Rome. In 42 B.C. the triumvirate was troubled by some of Antony's forces fighting those of Octavian in Italy. In the tradition of the day, Antony, back in Rome, made peace with Octavian by marrying his daughter Octavia. The differences between the two ex-partners, however, continued to fester. Possibly anticipating a break with Octavian, Antony renewed his interest in Cleopatra. He invited her to meet him at Antioch in Syria. Cleopatra agreed and, although there is no record of their meeting, they apparently renewed their relationship. Though no wedding is recorded, they may even have married—in letters Antony referred to her as his wife. Afterward, Antony was soon off fighting Parthians and Armenians to hold his share, the eastern section, of the Roman empire.

Meanwhile, Lepidus had retired, leaving Octavian and Antony to quarrel about who ruled Rome. These two broke the union in 33 B.C., when Antony divorced Octavia. He and Cleopatra then began to recruit a multiethnic army, comprising Arabic, Jewish, Sudanese, Persian, Gaulish, and Roman soldiers, to battle Octavian.

At first Antony had some strong support from Rome. Four hundred of the twelve hundred senators left Rome and joined him in Asia Minor. These supporters, however, presented a problem. Cleopatra had her eyes on a monarchy in Rome ruled by Caesarion; Antony's Roman supporters wanted to restore the republic. Finally, Antony sided with his supporters from Rome and promised to recreate a republican government.

Propaganda war. In 31 B.C. Octavian began to use Cleopatra in a smear campaign to ensure Rome's support. He portrayed her as an Egyptian tyrant and a worshipper of animal gods. The Romans responded to this propaganda, and this enabled Octavian to eventually declare war on Cleopatra, but not on Antony.

▲ The Battle of Actium; at the height of the battle, Cleopatra VII suddenly withdrew her sixty ships and headed back to Egypt.

Meanwhile, Antony had moved to Athens, where he spent much of his time carousing and drinking. Disgusted with him and with the ever present Cleopatra, many of his Roman supporters began to desert him to join Octavian.

Defeat of Antony and Cleopatra. In 31 B.C. Octavian invaded western Greece and marched to the Gulf of Ambracia, where his fleet blockaded Antony's. Antony's supporters, based on shore at Actium, wanted to withdraw inland, but Cleopatra had more confidence in the navy. These included sixty of her own ships; she preferred to run the blockade. Antony agreed and the two navies joined in the Battle of Actium. At the height of the battle, Cleopatra suddenly withdrew her sixty ships and headed back to Egypt. Antony saw this and immediately left the battle in a single fast ship to join her. The two returned to Alexandria while Antony's forces were overwhelmed by those of Octavian. Octavian then sailed for Alexandria with his army. Seeing that their remaining forces were no match for Octavian's, Antony and Cleopatra committed suicide to avoid capture. Octavian later captured Caesarion and had him executed. It was the end of the Ptolemaic dynasty and of Cleopatra's plan to rule both Egypt and Rome.

Aftermath

Octavian in Egypt. Ironically, the Egypto-Roman empire ruled by a Caesar dynasty, which Cleopatra had wanted, came into being as a result of her death. Although Romans hailed him as the conqueror of Egypt, Octavian did not make it a Roman province. Though he was never actually crowned, Octavian took over as Cleopatra's successor with the blessing of the Egyptian priesthood. (Egyptians, after all, had accepted Caesar as Cleopatra's husband, and Octavian was his heir.) Octavian's successors were hailed as "pharaoh" in Egyptian writings. According to historian Arthur Weigall, "all of the Emperors of Rome came to be recognized in Egypt not as subjects of a foreign empire of which Egypt was a part, but as actual Pharaohs of Egyptian dominions of which Rome was a part" (Weigall, p. 435).

Emperors as gods. Cleopatra and Egypt may have influenced the development of the Roman empire and Western civilization in another way. The Roman emperors who succeeded Octavian ruled with absolute power and demanded that they be worshipped as gods. Even after the Roman empire and Western Europe became Christian, the idea that kings rule by divine right, which would have been considered a disgraceful idea by the Roman republicans, would persist for centuries.

For More Information

Barrow, R. H. *The Romans.* Hammondsworth, England: Penguin, 1968.

Langguth, A. J. *A Noise of War.* New York: Simon and Schuster, 1994.

Tarn, W. W. *Hellenistic Civilization.* 3rd edition, revised. Cleveland, Ohio: Meridian Books, 1961.

Weigall, Arthur. *The Life and Times of Cleopatra, Queen of Egypt.* New York: Putnam, 1924.

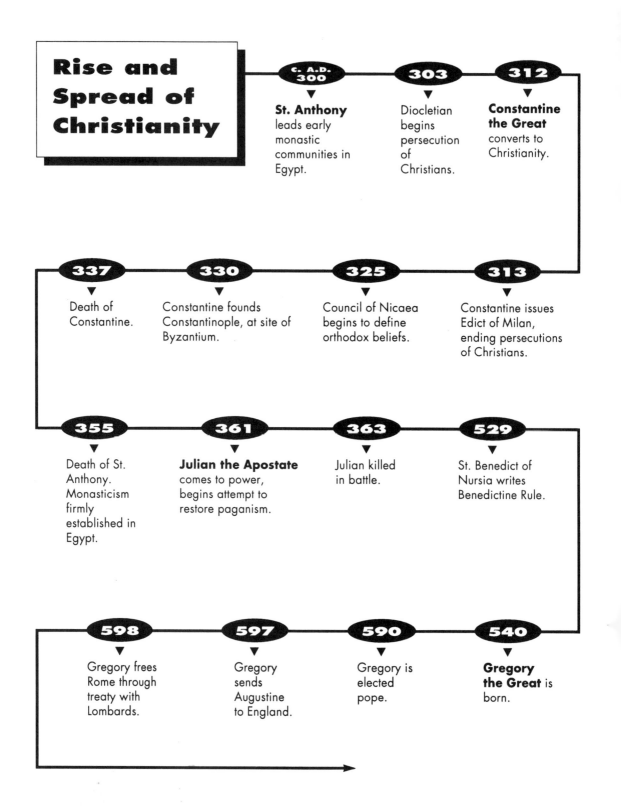

Rise and Spread of Christianity

c. A.D. 300
▼
St. Anthony leads early monastic communities in Egypt.

303
▼
Diocletian begins persecution of Christians.

312
▼
Constantine the Great converts to Christianity.

337
▼
Death of Constantine.

330
▼
Constantine founds Constantinople, at site of Byzantium.

325
▼
Council of Nicaea begins to define orthodox beliefs.

313
▼
Constantine issues Edict of Milan, ending persecutions of Christians.

355
▼
Death of St. Anthony. Monasticism firmly established in Egypt.

361
▼
Julian the Apostate comes to power, begins attempt to restore paganism.

363
▼
Julian killed in battle.

529
▼
St. Benedict of Nursia writes Benedictine Rule.

598
▼
Gregory frees Rome through treaty with Lombards.

597
▼
Gregory sends Augustine to England.

590
▼
Gregory is elected pope.

540
▼
Gregory the Great is born.

RISE AND SPREAD OF CHRISTIANITY

The third century A.D. was a time of crisis for the Roman empire. From the north, populous tribes of Germanic barbarians were constantly trying to take over desirable Roman territory. On the economic front, high inflation made cash less valuable and often forced common people to barter (trade) for food and goods. The army held the government captive, choosing and overthrowing emperors whenever the soldiers felt like it.

All these problems added up to a spiritual crisis as well. With little that they could count on in their daily lives, people turned to superstition for comfort. Magicians and fortune-tellers were consulted more than ever (though they had always been around in Roman society), and a number of so-called "mystery" religions or cults gained popularity.

Many of these cults were from the Middle East, especially the area between today's Syria and Egypt. Cults of the gods Mithras, Isis, and Serapis were among the most popular. Christianity, springing from the same region, shared some characteristics with the mystery cults: secret rituals, for example, and a belief in personal salvation for the soul in an afterlife. Such beliefs in a better world to come offered comfort to people faced with a world that was often unstable and unpleasant.

Christianity, however, had one important difference: like the Jewish religion from which it sprang, Christianity did not recognize gods other than its own. This brought it into direct conflict with the Roman government. Rome required people to worship the traditional state gods and above all to worship the emperor, who was himself seen as a god.

Many Christians were tortured and killed for their refusal to worship the emperor. They became the martyrs of the early church. *Martus*, the Greek word for "witness," eventually became the English word "martyr." Thus these Christian martyrs were literally "witnesses" to their own faith—that is, they publicly refused to give it up, even under torture. Such strong beliefs impressed people, and the ranks of the Christians grew, despite persecutions in which the state tried to stamp the Christians out.

The worst persecutions occurred during the reign of Diocletian, who ruled the Roman empire from 284 to 305. Yet it was Diocletian's successor, **Constantine the Great,** who changed everything by adopting Christianity himself. Constantine not only repealed the old anti-Christian laws but also passed new laws giving the church special advantages (such as not having to pay taxes, for example). Church membership now grew rapidly.

Though Christianity would in time replace paganism (the traditional non-Christian beliefs) as the state religion, this slow process took many years. Constantine's own nephew **Julian the Apostate** rejected Christianity. During his short reign (361-362), Julian tried to restore worship of the pagan gods, but by this time, Christianity had become firmly established. Christians saw Julian's early death as a punishment from God. Julian was the empire's last pagan emperor.

As it changed the Roman state, Christianity was itself changed. During the century following the beginning of Constantine's reign, the church grew from a half-secret organization into an official, state-supported institution. Its beliefs, therefore, had to be defined and brought into some sort of uniformity. Bishops in the great Egyptian city of Alexandria, for example, had to agree with bishops in the new capital, Constantinople, on basic issues important to the church. Only then could the church claim to be "catholic," or universal.

Constantine and his successors took a major part in this process, holding a series of councils in which such issues were decided. Beginning with the Council of Nicaea in 325, these meetings established church orthodoxy ("right belief"). The emperor's role thus became central to church affairs.

Balancing this new public, official side of the church were movements that stressed Christianity's private, personal side. The most important of these was monasticism, or the practice of being a monk. (Most of the world's major religions have similar traditions.) Christian monasticism took root in Egypt under **St. Anthony.**

In search of a simple life that would be like the life led by Jesus Christ, Anthony went off to live in the desert. There he practiced asceticism, or disciplined self-denial, which he believed would strengthen his soul and his Christian faith. Others followed his example, and soon there were loosely organized communities of "hermits" seeking solitude in the desert under Anthony's leadership. From these beginnings, monasticism would eventually spread throughout both the eastern and western parts of the empire.

From Rome to Byzantium

In converting to Christianity and establishing a new capital, Constantinople, Constantine in effect founded a new empire. Called Byzantium after the old Greek trading town on which Constantinople was built, this new empire was based on Roman law but became Christian in its religion and Greek in its culture. Although Roman power crumbled in the West in the fifth century A.D., it survived in the Greek East until 1453. Conquered in that year by the invading Turks, Constantinople today is Istanbul, Turkey's major city.

Despite Constantine's efforts, Christianity was still ill-prepared for a great expansion. Church government was ineffective in either spreading the gospel or in protecting it. Although missionaries traveled across Europe and Asia soon after the church was founded, it was left to a simple monk, Benedict of Nursia, to devise in 529 a written code of behavior for religious authority and to begin to develop a structure for the outreaching church. Nearly three centuries after Constantine and half a century after Benedict, **Gregory the Great,** the first medieval pope, followed the Benedictine Code to organize the church in Italy, reduce its enemies, and reinvigorate the role of missionaries.

St. Anthony

c. 250-355

Personal Background

Anthony was born in a small town in Egypt, partway up the Nile River, sometime around 250. In ancient times, as now, settlement in Egypt was mostly limited to a thin strip of land along the Nile. There the river brought water for irrigation, along with the rich layer of soil that was laid down each spring by the river's yearly flood. Outside of this narrow strip, for hundreds of miles on either side, stretched the vast expanse of the Egyptian desert. Hot, dry, and inhospitable, its rocky hills and dusty plains promised only hardship, loneliness, and discomfort to anyone who might think of living there. And few did—until Anthony, who had his own reasons for seeking the challenges of living in the desert.

Christian family. Anthony's parents were prosperous, upper-class Egyptians. They had plenty of money for the finer things in life, and the household never lacked for food or clothing. But they were also Christians, which meant that they tried to live more simply than others of their social standing. Raised as a Christian, Anthony went to church with his parents, and always paid close attention to the lessons that the priests read to the churchgoers.

Home life. When it came time for him to go to school, however, Anthony did not respond with the same enthusiasm. The lessons there did not grip him like the Bible stories and sermons

▲ **St. Anthony, in detail from**
The Temptation of St. Anthony, **1509,**
by Lucas van Leyden.

Event: Development of monasticism.

Role: An Egyptian Christian, Anthony lived a hermit's life in the desert, wanting to be alone in thought and religious contemplation. Soon, however, he attracted followers, whom he organized into the first communities of Christian "monks"—those who lived a "monastic" or solitary life.

he heard at church. And he showed little desire to play with other children, preferring instead a quiet life at home. There he was very happy. Unlike most children, he never asked for things from his parents. He didn't want lots of toys and never demanded any special foods or desserts. As his biographer St. Athanasius reported, "He was satisfied with what was put before him, and asked no more" (Athanasius, p. 19).

Participation: Development of Monasticism

Hearing the call. Anthony's parents died when he was about eighteen or twenty years old, leaving him and his sister, who was very young. One day soon after his parents' death, as he was on his way to church, he started thinking about parts of the Bible that have to do with money and possessions. The Apostles, for example, gave up everything they had in order to follow Christ. And as he entered the church, he heard the priest read the following passage from the Bible, in which Jesus speaks to a rich man: "If thou wilt [wish] be perfect, go sell what thou hast [owns], and give to the poor, and thou shalt have treasure in Heaven" (Matthew 19:21).

Athanasius and Anthony

The information about St. Anthony's life in this article comes from his younger friend Athanasius, who wrote *The Life of St. Anthony* just after Anthony's death. Athanasius was bishop of Alexandria, Egypt's leading city. He played an important role in defining the beliefs of the Christian church during the fourth century, and the church declared him a saint after his death in 373.

Anthony took the words seriously. He went back outside and, without any hesitation, simply gave all the land he had inherited from his parents to the people of the town. He sold everything else and gave the money to the poor, keeping a little for his sister.

Tomorrow's cares. He returned to church, but as he entered he heard the priest read out more of Jesus's words: "Be ... not anxious about tomorrow; for tomorrow will be anxious about the things of itself" (Matthew 6:34). So he left again, gave away the money he had kept for his little sister, and placed her in the care of nuns. Anthony wanted to follow the words of Jesus and let tomorrow's cares worry about themselves. He believed it was not up to him to look out for his sister; rather it was up to God to look out for both of them, and up to him to accept whatever God decided.

Search. However, Anthony did not believe that he should just remain idle, because the Bible also said, "If any would not work, neither should he eat" (2 Thessalonians 3:10). Over the next few years, Anthony worked at whatever jobs were available, spending what he needed on food and giving away the rest. He also began seeking out Christian men who were living the kind of life that he wanted to live. Called "ascetics," such men denied themselves comforts and luxuries, hoping to improve their souls by disciplining their minds and bodies.

One ascetic, for example, might go without food or might sleep on the ground. Another would keep up long hours of study and meditation. Yet another might be known for his constant generosity or cheerfulness. As he visited them, Anthony learned the special lesson that each man had to offer. Having seen them in action, he then returned and tried to imitate the qualities that made each of them stand out. He also prayed constantly and, of course, continued to attend church.

> ## Tales of Demons and Heroes
>
> Athanasius' *Life of St. Anthony* became a model for later works about saints' lives. Most likely true in its basic outlines, it seems meant to reveal Christian beliefs and to portray a saint's perfection, rather than always to give the literal facts of Anthony's life. The tales of Anthony and the devil, which take up much of the work, may especially be seen in this light. Whether they are true or not, they point out the values that gave Christianity its wide appeal. Such tales also show the saints in action as the young religion's heroes.

Temptation. Athanasius wrote that when Anthony's simple life had won him the love of all who knew him, the devil decided it was time to send some trouble Anthony's way. First, said Athanasius, the devil tried to make him feel guilty about deserting his sister and reminded him of all the pleasures he was missing. When that didn't work, the devil came in the night as an attractive woman to tempt him with thoughts of sex. But Anthony refused to be tempted, and the devil left him alone—for the time being. According to Athanasius, this was Anthony's first victory over the devil.

Demons. After his first victory over temptation, Anthony went to spend time alone in the tombs, large caverns used for burials, that lay outside of town. Asking a friend to bring him some bread from time to time, he entered one of the tombs and locked the door. He stayed alone inside.

This, wrote Athanasius, was too much for the devil, who now feared that Anthony:

> would fill the desert ... with his asceticism [self-denial]. So [the devil] came one night with a great number of demons and lashed [Anthony] so unmercifully that he lay on the ground speechless from the pain. [Anthony] maintained that the pain was so severe that the blows could not have been inflicted by any man and cause such agony. (Athanasius, pp. 26-27)

Anthony, Athanasius continued, held out against the demons until finally God came to him and chased them away. "Where were you?" Anthony asked. "Why did you not appear at the beginning to stop my pains?" And a voice came to him, "Anthony, I was right here, but I waited to see you in action. And now, because you held out and did not surrender, I will ever be your helper and I will make you renowned [famous] everywhere." (Athanasius, p. 29)

Into the desert. Soon after that, Anthony—fired with new enthusiasm for the ascetic life—went to one of the men he earlier had visited. He asked the man to come live with him in the desert. The man, who was very old, refused. So Anthony set off into the desert by himself. He made his way to a place called Pispir, east of the Nile about fifty miles south of Memphis. There, on the rugged slopes of an isolated mountain, he found an old deserted fort. With a six-month supply of bread and water, he blocked up the entrance and disappeared inside. About thirty-five at this time Anthony would spend almost twenty years living in the old fort on the mountain, receiving bread twice a year from his only neighbor, a farmer who lived nearby.

"Father and guide." By the end of this period, Anthony's determination and self-control were well known throughout the Christian community in Egypt. Many other Christians wanted to follow his example and take up the ascetic life. Finally, eager for his leadership, one group came and broke down his door. Anthony emerged, looking just as he had before going in, which surprised

◄
Temptation of St. Anthony **by Matthias Grünewald, detail from the**
Isenheim Altarpiece, **completed in 1515.**

those who had expected him to be pale and sickly from lack of food and fresh air. When he saw the large crowd that had gathered, he greeted them warmly and with his usual charm. He spoke to them, urging them to do as he had done, to give up the needs of the body for the needs of the soul. And many did, finding caves or other simple dwellings nearby or elsewhere in the desert.

These dwellings were the first Christian monasteries, and those who lived in them were the first monks, or *monachoi* in Greek—"those who are alone." "And soon," Athanasius wrote, "as his message drew men after him, the number of monasteries multiplied and to all he was father and guide" (Athanasius, p. 33).

Martyrs in Alexandria. In 311, when Anthony was in his early sixties, the Roman government once again began to arrest Christians. As with such persecutions in the past, many were tried and executed for refusing to worship the emperor. Anthony went north to Alexandria, where officials were holding the martyrs, as other Christians called those who were to be executed because they refused to give up their faith and worship the emperor.

Anthony accompanied the martyrs to court, comforting them and staying with them as they were executed. He made no attempt at all to hide the fact that he was a Christian, too. In fact, Athanasius wrote, Anthony was praying to be a martyr himself. But God, Athanasius said, was saving Anthony for the important work of founding the Christian monastic tradition.

Inner Mountain. Anthony returned to his mountain near Pispir, but he had become so famous that it was difficult for him to find the solitude that his faith demanded. Followers knocked on his door constantly, along with the sick or those with sick loved ones, for it was widely believed that Anthony had the power to heal the sick. And many who came to him were healed, Athanasius wrote, although Anthony always said that it was God—and their own faith—that really healed them.

In order to be alone, Anthony finally had to search for a new site, much farther away from everything. After traveling through the desert for three days, he found another mountain, deep in the desert about seventy-five miles east of the Nile. Surrounded by flat desert, it rose high out of the plains, with a good source of water at its base. Anthony, Athanasius reported, "fell in love with the place" (Athanasius, p. 62). His followers called it the Inner Mountain to set it apart from his old site, which they called the Outer Mountain.

Letter from Constantine. Now an old man, Anthony spent the rest of his life at the Inner Mountain, where he grew a few vegetables in a simple garden and gave himself over to prayer and meditation. He made regular trips to the sites of other monks, to offer tips and advice on how best to live the life they had chosen. The emperor **Constantine** (see entry), the first Roman emperor to become a Christian himself, "wrote to him as to a father and begged him to write back" (Athanasius, p. 86). Many also visited him to seek advice or to bring food and do a little work for their aging "brother." Some of his visitors were Greek philosophers, non-Christians who wanted to argue with the famous monk. As Athanasius told it, they always went away impressed by Anthony's wisdom, even though he had had little education.

Aftermath

Death. By the time of his death in 355, hundreds of monks lived the ascetic life, in "cells" around the desert or in communities such as that which had sprung up at Anthony's original site at Pispir. When he felt that he was ready to die, Anthony called for the two younger monks who lived with him because of his old age. Asking them never to reveal his burial place, he said that he wanted to leave two of his simple garments, a sheepskin and a cape, to Athanasius, who had given them to him. He left one or two other items—another sheepskin and a "hair shirt" (made of leather with the fur still on the inside for discomfort)—to others. He then quietly died.

For More Information

Athanasius, St. *The Life of St. Anthony.* Translated and with notes by Robert T. Meyer. New York: Newman Press, 1950.

MacMullen, Ramsay. *Christianizing the Roman Empire.* New Haven, Connecticut: Yale University Press, 1984.

The Student Bible. New International Version. Grand Rapids, Michigan: Zondervan, 1992.

Constantine the Great

c. 288-337

Personal Background

We know that Flavius Valerius Constantinus, called Constantine in English, was born in February, probably on the twenty-seventh, though the exact date and the year are uncertain. His birthplace, also uncertain, was probably Naissus, a city in the Roman province of Illyria (present-day Nis, in what is now Serbia).

Up through the ranks. Constantine's father, Constantius Chlorus, was an Illyrian soldier who had risen through the ranks to become a high official in the Roman government. Like other peoples of the Roman provinces, many Illyrians served in the Roman army, which was the main path to getting ahead in the government. Well liked by his troops, Constantius was a good general, a powerfully built, red-faced man whose own father had been a goat herder. Constantine's mother, Helena, was a waitress—or perhaps the owner, as some sources claim—at a local inn.

At the emperor's court. When Constantine was a boy of perhaps nine or ten, he was sent away to be raised at the court of the new emperor Diocletian. Like Constantius, Diocletian was a peasant's son from the provinces, in Diocletian's case Dalmatia (present-day coastal Croatia). Also like Constantius, Diocletian had risen through the ranks to a high position in the army. The two had long been political allies, and Constantius had supported Diocletian, who became emperor in the year 284. Constantine was

▲ Constantine the Great

Event: The Roman empire accepts Christianity.

Role: As the first Roman emperor who was also a Christian, Constantine not only made his religion legal but linked it firmly to the government itself. Earlier emperors had arrested and executed Christians, but under Constantine the church, now growing in membership, enjoyed the protection of the Roman state.

educated at Diocletian's court, where he learned about power and politics.

Tetrarchy. Diocletian came to power after a century of great troubles for the empire. To help deal with these problems, he created the "tetrarchy," or "rule by four." He divided the empire into two halves, each with a senior emperor and a junior emperor. Diocletian, who took over as senior emperor of the eastern half, appointed Constantius junior emperor of the western half in 293.

Pronunciation Key

Constantius: kon **stan** chee us

Constantine: **kon** stan teen

Diocletian: dye uh **klee** shun

Byzantine: **bih** zan teen

Byzantium: bih **zan** tee um

For several years, Constantine remained at the court of Diocletian. Though officially at Nicomedia (Izmit in present-day Turkey), the court usually traveled around with the emperor and the army. It had been years since the emperor remained in Rome, and military duties along the frontiers had led most emperors to govern from wherever they happened to be at the time. With German tribes threatening invasion from the north and the Persian empire pressing in the east, emperors had to be good soldiers, ready to move their troops rapidly to any trouble spot. When he was about twenty, Constantine himself joined the army, serving under Diocletian and then under Galerius, the junior emperor in the east.

Participation:
The Roman Empire Accepts Christianity

Persecution. In 303 Diocletian issued an order that Christian churches be torn down and Bibles and other Christian holy writings be burned. Public officials who admitted to being Christian were supposed to be dismissed from their jobs, and bishops and other church officials imprisoned and killed. Constantine himself was not yet a Christian. Like his father, he worshipped the traditional gods. Still, he was not anti-Christian, and he later said that Diocletian's order shocked him. The order was not carried out everywhere. Constantine's father, for example, who was posted in Britain, did not put it into effect. It was mostly in the empire's eastern part that bishops and others were imprisoned,

▲ Rome under Constantine, circa 324; six years later he would found a "New Rome" and name it after himself.

tortured, and executed. Such persecutions had happened before, under other emperors, but this was by far the worst. As it turned out, though, it would be the last.

Diocletian retires. In 305 Diocletian retired, forcing his fellow senior emperor to do the same. One of his main goals in creating the tetrarchy had been to provide a stable way for new emperors to take office. The junior emperors were next in line, and so Constantius now took over as senior emperor in the West. This left the two places open for junior emperors, and many thought that Constantine would be one of those chosen by the retiring

Diocletian (who had always held the real power). But Diocletian passed Constantine over, choosing another young officer instead.

Constantine now left for the West, joining his father in Britain in 306. Only a month or two after Constantine's arrival, Constantius died. That was long enough, however, for Constantine to become popular among his father's men. Constantius's loyal troops immediately hailed Constantine as emperor in his father's place.

Family Politics

In 307 Constantine divorced his first wife, Minervina, to marry Maxentius's sister, Fausta, creating an alliance that was supposed to improve relations between the two ambitious generals. Constantine had a son, Crispus, by Minervina and three sons—Constantine II, Constantius II, and Constans—and a daughter, Constantia, by Fausta. All of his sons followed Constantine into the army, and all but Crispus ruled as co-emperors after Constantine's death. One the deepest mysteries in Constantine's rule occurred in 326, when he had Fausta and Crispus killed, supposedly on a charge of treason, though details remain unknown.

Civil wars. Without Diocletian's personal presence on the scene, the tetrarchy now completely broke down. Like Constantine, there were others who thought they had a claim to be one of the emperors. Maxentius, for example, the son of the Western emperor who had been forced to retire with Diocletian, had also been passed over. He now made the same claim as Constantine, that he was rightful senior emperor of the West. Others made similar claims, and there followed a long period of civil war as the competing and ambitious generals fought it out.

By 310 control of the West had come down to either Maxentius or Constantine. Others had fallen away in four years of battles and political conflict. Constantine's position was stronger than ever, but he had to keep putting down rebellions by the tribes occupying Roman territory in Gaul (present-day France), as well as fighting off invasions by those living beyond Roman borders.

Apollo and Sol. It was at this point that Constantine had the first of several reported visions, or religious experiences seeming to contain a special message from a divine being. Sometime in 310, as he was marching his army north to take care of business along the border, the god Apollo appeared to Constantine, so the story goes, promising him victory and thirty years of unchallenged rule. Apollo was also associated with another god, the sun-god Sol, known as Sol Invictus, or "the Unconquered Sun." After

▲ *The Apparition of the Cross to Constantine* by Giulio Romano. While the tales concerning Constantine's conversion were most likely made up years later, the victory that followed certainly was not.

his vision, Constantine began to link himself to these gods in his public statements.

For example, Apollo and Sol began showing up on coins issued by Constantine. In an age without television or newspapers, coins were an important way of spreading a leader's image. Constantine chose "the Unconquered Sun" to appear on the opposite side of the coin from his own portrait, showing his desire to seem invincible and powerful.

"With this sign you will conquer." By 312 Constantine, based in northern Europe, was ready for a showdown with Maxentius, whose base was the empire's old capital, Rome. That summer Constantine invaded Italy from the north, though his generals had advised against it. Maxentius's army in Rome was large, perhaps twice Constantine's forty thousand men. Yet Maxentius was an unpopular ruler, and the cities of northern Italy offered little resistance as Constantine moved southward with his men.

Details differ according to which writer told the story, but sometime before reaching Rome, Constantine is said to have had another vision. One afternoon a blazing cross appeared in the sky. Around it were the words, "With this sign you will conquer." According to the story, the whole army saw it. That night, Jesus Christ appeared to Constantine in a dream and told him to use the cross as his guardian in battle.

Conversion and victory. Such were the tales surrounding perhaps the most significant event in the history of the Christian church, Constantine's conversion to Christianity. Yet in reality, we know nothing of what led Constantine to take up Christian beliefs. While the tales were most likely made up years later, the victory that followed certainly was not. On October 28, 313, at the battle of the Milvian Bridge outside Rome, Constantine routed Maxentius, who was killed in the fighting. Constantine was now unchallenged ruler of the Western empire. And events would soon show that, as far as he was concerned, he owed his victory not to Apollo or Sol, but to the Christian God.

Toleration. Despite his belief that the Christian God had helped him win, Constantine seems to have become fully Christian not overnight but over the next ten years or so. Soon after his victory in the West, in 313, he and Licinius, now the Eastern emperor, published the "Edict of Milan," a law officially ending the persecutions started under Diocletian. The law also called for greater religious toleration in general, though it didn't actually mention Christians by name. Soon afterward, Constantine's belief that the Christian God had helped him win power led him to begin giving Christians special protection and privileges under the government. Later, he gave government money to help build churches in various cities and towns of the West.

▲ The Council of Nicaea, the first council convened by Constantine the Great to solve the problems of the church.

Final victory. As Constantine built up his power in the West, it became clear that, as earlier with Maxentius, a showdown with Licinius was unavoidable. It finally came in 324. By then Constantine had firmly established his ties to the church. With the Christians becoming ever stronger in society as their numbers grew, he used these ties for his own political advantage. By painting Licinius as anti-Christian (which he probably was not), Constantine succeeded in turning the coming conflict into a religious crusade. He thus cleverly won the publicity war, and with his military skills won the actual war, which came in February 324. By September, with Licinius's surrender at Nicomedia in present-day Turkey, Constantine had won control of the whole Roman empire.

Dreams of a universal church. Even before his victory over Licinius, Constantine had begun taking a role in church affairs. Beginning in 315, he had tried his hardest to settle an internal church dispute known as the Donatist controversy. The issue was how the church should view those who had given up Christianity during the persecutions. Some refused to let them back into the church, while others thought they should be forgiven. Still a newcomer to the faith, Constantine brought leading Christians to his court to advise him. Despite his best attempts, however, he only met with frustration in trying to get the two sides to agree.

When the church had been a small, half-secret operation, it hadn't mattered as much if Christians in one city believed exactly what those elsewhere believed. Now that it was openly growing under imperial protection, however, official church positions had to be clarified. Constantine wanted a "catholic," or universal, church with a single set of rules and doctrines. He also believed that his position as emperor should command the respect of the church leaders who were arguing over what course the church should take. Now, his control over the whole empire secure, Constantine prepared to take an even stronger role in settling disputes within the church.

Council of Nicaea. Early in 325, therefore, Constantine called a council of bishops (high officials of the church) in the city of Nicaea, in present-day Turkey. A division of Christians was taking place in Egypt over disagreements about the exact nature of Christ. Arius, a priest from Alexandria, Egypt's leading city, claimed that Christ was basically human: God the Father had created Christ (God the Son), he said, and therefore Christ was not "eternal" like God the Father. Other powerful bishops disagreed, claiming that Christ was basically divine and had always existed just like God the Father. The debate spread throughout Christianity. Those called to Nicaea were to arbitrate the disagreement.

With Constantine acting as chairman, the council decided that Arius was wrong. In the so-called "Nicene Creed," as its decision is known, it is said that Christ was basically divine. Arius and his followers were heretics (holders of unorthodox opinions), the council declared, Christians who followed teachings that went against official church beliefs. Yet Arius's followers continued to put forward their beliefs and to win new followers anyway. Indeed, this and other disputes over beliefs continue to plague the church to this day. It was easier, Constantine had found, to control a roomful of arguing bishops than a "universal" church of different peoples with widely differing beliefs.

Aftermath

Christian empire. Constantine ruled for another twelve years, until his death in 337. By then Christianity—rapidly growing now—had become firmly established as the empire's most influential religion. Only one non-Christian emperor would come after Constantine, and within a century Christianity would become the official religion of the Roman state. Following Constantine's example, emperors would share religious authority with the highest church officials.

In 330 Constantine founded Constantinople, a new capital for the empire, a "New Rome" named after its founder. Set on the site of an ancient Greek trading town called Byzantium and today known as Istanbul, Turkey. Constantinople proved an excellent choice. For more than one thousand years, it survived as the capital of a new Christian state, the Byzantine empire, that evolved out of the eastern part of the Roman empire in the years following Constantine's death.

For More Information

Cameron, Averil. *The Later Roman Empire.* Cambridge, Massachusetts: Harvard University Press, 1993.

Grant, Michael. *Constantine the Great.* New York: Macmillan, 1993.

MacMullen, Ramsay. *Constantine.* New York: Dial Press, 1969.

Julian the Apostate

c. 331-363

Personal Background

The man whom Christians would call "the Apostate" (one who "stands away" from or gives up a religion) was born into the Roman empire's ruling family during the reign of his uncle, **Constantine the Great** (see entry). His name was Flavius Claudius Julianus, or Julian in English; his father, Julius, was the emperor's half-brother.

Mistrust. Relations within the imperial family were tense, partly because marriages and divorces had sometimes been made for political reasons. For example, Constantine's father, the emperor Constantius I, had divorced his mother, Helena, to make a political marriage to Theodora, Julius's mother. Consequently, Helena hated Theodora and her children. She and Constantine feared that they might try to seize power for themselves. Julius had long been kept imprisoned (though comfortably) in a remote country house far from the centers of power. By the 330s, however, he was allowed to move to the new capital, Constantinople, recently founded by Constantine. There Julian was born, in May or June of 331 or 332.

Murder. Suspicions again came to a boiling point when Constantine died in 337. His three sons, who didn't trust each other much, wanted to make sure that no one could threaten their claims to the throne. One of them, Constantius II, spread a rumor

▲ **Julian the Apostate**

Event: Attempt to revive paganism.

Role: The nephew of the first Christian Roman emperor Constantine, Julian was the only non-Christian emperor to rule after his uncle. Though raised as a Christian, he abandoned that faith as an adult. As emperor, he tried to restore traditional pagan worship as society's chief religion, but his reign was cut short by his death at age thirty-two.

that when Constantine had died, he had accused Julius of poisoning him. Constantine's troops, who had loved him greatly, rushed to Julius's palace and killed both him and Julian's oldest brother. Another brother, Gallus, sick and thought to be dying, was spared. Five-year-old Julian, so the story went, was spared because he was so young.

Exile. Julian's mother had died when he was only a few months old, so the boy was now an orphan. It is not known whether he actually saw the soldiers kill his father and brother. Even if he didn't see them, though, the events of that night must have left him terrified.

Julian spent the rest of his boyhood in comfortable but sometimes lonely exile. From the age of about six to twelve he lived at one of his grandmother's houses in Nicomedia, not far from Constantinople. There he developed a love of books, encouraged by his tutor, Mardonius. The two grew close, and in the future Julian would always think of Mardonius as having raised him.

The years in Nicomedia were happy ones on the whole, and at twelve Julian was saddened to hear that he could no longer live there with Mardonius. Constantine's sons had finally begun to war among themselves openly for the throne. Constantius II, whose base was the capital, had decided that Julian was too much of a possible threat in Nicomedia. So Julian was taken south, to a luxurious hunting lodge in Cappadocia, deep in the heart of Asia Minor (present-day Turkey). There, with a few books, new teachers, and no friends, he passed the rest of his boyhood.

Participation: Attempt to Revive Paganism

Pagan traditions. Like the rest of the imperial family, Julian was brought up as a Christian. Only recently, after it was adopted by Constantine, had Christianity come out into the open. Before, it had been a half-secret religion, whose followers were often persecuted. Only a generation earlier, under the emperor Diocletian, who ruled just before Constantine, the worst persecutions ever had taken place. Churches were torn down, and Christians were tortured and executed. Now, though, the tables had turned. The

▲ Julian the Apostate depicted on a coin of his reign. As emperor, Julian
could finally drop his Christian mask and come out into the open as a
pagan.

Christian church enjoyed special privileges and a rapidly growing
membership under imperial protection.

It was too early, however, for Christians to have set up many
of the educational institutions that would later follow. Instead,
they still relied largely on pagan schools and pagan educational
traditions. In 349, when Julian was about eighteen, Constantius II
(who had won the power struggle with his brothers) allowed his
young cousin to attend some of these schools.

Secret beliefs. For the following six years, Julian studied in
the old Greek centers of learning. It was the happiest time of his
life. In Athens and the other Greek cities, pagan religious beliefs

had become closely linked to the ideas of ancient philosophers such as Plato. By the end of this period, Julian had grown fascinated by these traditional beliefs and the philosophical ideas that went with them. He rejected Christianity and embraced the old ways instead—but his situation as a member of the imperial family was dangerous. He had to hide his decision. To stay alive, he pretended to remain Christian.

Junior emperor. Meanwhile, Constantius needed an assistant, a junior emperor, to look after the western part of the empire while he himself responded to a threat from Persia in the east. In 351 he had chosen Julian's surviving brother, Gallus, for the job. Gallus had been with Julian in Cappadocia, but the two had little in common. While Julian was quiet and studious, loving his world of books and ideas, Gallus had little patience with such distractions.

In 354, suspecting that Gallus had ambitions for the throne, Constantius had him executed. Late the following year, the emperor chose a family member to replace Gallus—one who would never be a threat to his own power: Gallus's intellectual, mild-mannered younger brother, Julian.

Success in Gaul. Summoning the startled Julian to Constantinople, Constantius raised him to the rank of junior emperor and gave him responsibility for protecting Roman territory in Gaul. (Gaul was the Roman province comprising present-day France, Switzerland, and southern Germany.) In the traditional way, Constantius presented the new commander to his troops. Stocky, awkward, with a sagging lower lip and an odd sideways tilt to his head, the inexperienced twenty-four-year-old was an uninspiring sight to the soldiers.

During the next five years, however, Julian proved himself to be a talented general, popular among both his men and the civilian population of Gaul. Often outnumbered more than two to one, he and his men defeated the invading Germanic tribes in several major battles. He then took the offensive, pushing north into German territory beginning in 358, where he restored Roman rule.

Rebellion in Paris. By early 360 Julian had the situation in Gaul firmly under control. Constantius, meanwhile, was having less success in the East. In January, he ordered Julian to send him reinforcements, demanding about two-thirds of Julian's troops. Julian was shocked. Not only would such a loss make it impossible to control Gaul any longer, it would break a promise that Julian had made to his men never to send them east. Most of them were romanized Gauls. They knew that if they went, they would probably never see their families again. Even if they survived the journey and the fighting in Persia and made it home, without the army's protection their families would be defenseless while they were gone.

Julian was at his army headquarters in Paris when the order came. He was no longer a timid student mainly concerned with keeping a low profile. Five years of command had given him self-confidence—and, it seems, ambition. As his angry troops gathered outside his quarters, he considered his choices. Meanwhile, the men outside threatened to run out of control. When they loudly proclaimed him senior emperor, equal to Constantius, Julian went along with them.

As often in the past, soldiers had made a Roman emperor. It now remained for the rebellious general to prove his right to rule by winning the civil war that was sure to follow.

"We worshipped the gods openly." By a stroke of luck, however, Julian never had to do so. While preparing to march against Julian from the Middle East, Constantius suddenly died. Julian, naturally, took his cousin's timely death as a sign of support from the gods. So, probably, did the soldiers in this age of superstition. Constantius's army immediately proclaimed Julian emperor, and the struggle was over before it had begun. In 361 Julian stood alone at the height of power.

Finally he could afford to drop his Christian mask and come out into the open as a pagan. As he wrote at the time in a letter to one of his old teachers: "We worshipped the gods openly, and most of the army which accompanied me reveres them. We sacrificed oxen in public. We offered many hecatombs [roasted-meat sacrifices] to the gods as expressions of thanks" (Bowersock, p. 61).

Reforms. Julian wasted no time in letting everybody know that he intended to make some real changes. First, he arrested many of Constantius's officials whom he thought had been guilty of misusing their positions. They were put on trial, and Julian made sure not to interfere in the verdicts of the court. He also cut back on the number of staff in the imperial household, getting rid of thousands of cooks, butlers, barbers, and others. More importantly, he increased the power of the senate in Constantinople, which had lost its influence as emperors governed more and more single-handedly.

Religious laws. Julian also passed laws that he thought would bring about the return of the worship of traditional gods. He repealed earlier laws that had forbidden old-style sacrifices, closed pagan temples, and confiscated pagan property. He didn't plan any persecutions and preferred instead to be tolerant of the Christians. All paganism needed, he believed, was an even chance. He did pardon all Christians who had been exiled during disputes within the church itself, allowing the exiles to return. This, he hoped, would create further conflict among the Christians and weaken the church.

Banning Christian teachers. The strongest measure that Julian took against the Christians was to ban them from jobs teaching the works of pagan writers. Since such writers—Plato, Aristotle, Homer, and others—made up all of what was taught in schools, in effect the law banned Christians from teaching. More than anything else he did as emperor, this law, which he passed in 362, brought Julian bitter protests from the Christians. Even one of Julian's main supporters, the pagan historian Ammianus, wrote that it "deserved to be buried in eternal silence" (Norwich, p. 362). Christians held protest demonstrations in many of the empire's major cities.

Sacrifices and sarcasm. In trying to restore pagan worship, Julian stressed such activities as public sacrifices of animals, at which the meat would be roasted and used to feed the crowd. At least, that was how the sacrifices had been done in earlier times. But times had changed, and such sacrifices were no longer popular. Nor were the complicated and often sarcastic documents that Julian wrote to attack his enemies. Such writings only served to hurt his support even among the pagans, who saw them as arrogant and self-serving.

Aftermath

Persian expedition. How such policies would have worked out will always remain a mystery. Julian was killed in battle in 363 while leading a military expedition against Persia, the empire's old enemy to the east. Some said it was a Christian from his own army who killed him, not a Persian. After his death, the army chose a Christian, Jovian, as his successor, and soon Julian's brief rule was no more than a temporary setback on the path to creating a fully Christian state, the Byzantine empire.

For More Information

Bowersock, G. W. *Julian the Apostate.* Cambridge, Massachusetts: Harvard University Press, 1978.

Browning, Robert. *The Emperor Julian.* Berkeley and Los Angeles: University of California Press, 1976.

Head, Constance. *The Emperor Julian.* Boston, Massachusetts: Twayne, 1976.

Norwich, John Julius. *Byzantium: The Early Centuries.* London: Penguin, 1990.

A Pagan Church?

One thing that allowed the Christian church to survive was its tight organization; one thing that made it attractive was its emphasis on moral virtue in daily behavior. Julian recognized these two strengths, and tried to give them to paganism. In contrast with pagan worship in the past, he seems to have envisioned an organized pagan church, similar to that of the Christians. And he also tried to give paganism a set of moral guidelines for virtuous behavior—something for which the old gods, with their love affairs and battles, were certainly never known.

Gregory the Great

c. 540-604

Personal Background

Early life. Much of what is known about Gregory is gathered directly from 850 of his own letters that have survived. The earliest account of his life is by Paul the Longobard, revised later by John the Deacon.

Gregory was born in Rome to Gordian and Sylvia, members of a prominent senatorial family. His family background emphasized scholarship and religious devotion, already having produced two popes, Felix III (reign 483-492) and Agapetus (reign 535-536). While still a young man, Gregory became known for his humility and generosity.

Administrator and monk. In his youth, Gregory considered the life of a priest in a monastery but postponed his move, thinking that he could best serve God as a judge. His accomplishments as a student of law resulted in his appointment in 570 as prefect (governor) of Rome. His duties included presiding over the Roman senate and managing the defense and charity services of the city. After his father's death, however, he renounced worldly possessions and earthly affairs. He used his great inheritance to fund the construction of six monasteries in Sicily and a seventh, dedicated to St. Andrew, on his family estate in Rome. In 575 he entered the order and the monastery he had built at his home on Monte Coelio in Rome. Because he had built the

▲ **Gregory the Great**

Event: Establishing papal power.

Role: Gregory the Great, also known as St. Gregory, is often considered the first medieval pope and is ranked with Ambrose, Jerome, and Augustine as one of the four "Doctors of the Church." Through his support of monasticism, commonsense theology, and missionary zeal, he prompted a change in papal relations with secular powers.

monastery, he might have entered monastic life as the abbot, or leader, but he preferred no favors and entered church service as a simple monk. His commitment to the Benedictine Order and a life of poverty was so great that he nearly destroyed his health.

Gregory was pulled back into public affairs in 578, when the pope made him one of Rome's seven cardinal deacons. He then went to Constantinople as an apocriarius (resident ambassador). Gregory served the church in Constantinople for seven years before returning to his monastery, this time as abbot.

A reluctant pope. Gregory returned to Rome in 579 as abbot of St. Andrew's and adviser to the pope. While he was there, plague struck Rome, claiming Pope Pelagius. By popular acclaim, in 590 Gregory was chosen the successor, despite his own hesitance. He even attempted to leave Rome so he would not be consecrated pope:

> He was unable to do so, because every gate was watched day and night to prevent him from escaping. Finally he won over certain traders, and they carried him out of the city in a tun [a large container]; and he took refuge in a cave in the depths of the woods, and there remained hidden for three days. (de Voragine, p. 179)

An empire divided. The decline of Roman imperial power following the death of **Constantine the Great** (see entry) in 337 A.D. contributed to the growing separation between the eastern and western parts of the empire. In the fourth century A.D., the sprawling empire was divided into two sections for administrative purposes, with the west maintaining Rome as its capital and the east taking Constantinople, or ancient Byzantium. By the late fifth century, the

The Influence of Benedict

Half a century before Gregory, Benedict of Nursia, a student in Rome, had become concerned about the disorganization and corruption in the city. He had at first fled the city to live alone, but his reputation spread and other concerned citizens soon joined him. Benedict established a set of rules to govern the assemblages of monks who came to follow him. Monasteries were to be completely controlled by their abbots under strict but gentle laws based on Biblical scripture. For example, Benedict allowed a would-be monk to stay in a monastery a year before taking an oath to lead a religious life. Benedict also gave dignity to manual labor by requiring monks to work to support the community. As a result, abbots and monks became powerful influences in their communities.

The monastery that Gregory constructed on his own home property was dedicated to the Benedictine Order, and Gregory patterned his own rule as abbot and later as pope after the guidelines set by Benedict.

West had fallen to migrating barbarian tribes who occupied the land, destroyed cities and countryside, disrupted communication and commerce, and threatened the empire's social and economic base. Thus by the sixth century, within the church, the Eastern emperor, a Greek, had difficulty relating to Latin-speaking Rome.

When a second wave of invaders, the pagan Lombards, took control of central and northern Italy in 569, they isolated Rome from the emperor in the Byzantine territories and even from the Eastern church's leaders in Ravenna in northeastern Italy. Though the provincial ruler at Ravenna lacked the military resources to fight, he refused to negotiate with the invading Lombards, fearing a treaty would legitimate their presence. The long-festering conflict proved an opportunity for Gregory to intervene and thus expand the powers of the church.

Participation: Establishing Papal Power

Eastern experience. Gregory's time in Constantinople had convinced him that the pope should pursue policies independent of the emperor and distant provincial governors. Already the pope had enough power to raise a formidable army. Avoiding both emperor and governor, Gregory dispatched his own troops and established a temporary truce with the Lombard dukes. The act established the church as an independent power to be reckoned with, and as the real ruling authority in Rome.

Regulation and reform. Gregory aimed to restore the church through the purity of its ministry. Combining his religious passion with his skill as an administrator, he began with the management of the papal properties—lands willed to the church in return for forgiveness of sins—in Sicily, Italy, and Provence (in present-day France). He appointed personal representatives to supervise and manage the lands, replacing the corrupt local officials who had routinely stolen from the land use revenues. Gregory held that the "recovered" income rightfully belonged to the poor; he used the moneys to provide food and clothes, run city services, and ransom prisoners. When Rome was under siege in 597, he used the money to protect the people by paying tribute to the Lombards.

Unification. Gregory held ultimate jurisdiction in church matters. His rule was tested when he reversed a decision of the patriarch (a senior church leader) at Constantinople. In an issue that demanded a decision concerning two priests, the patriarch claimed the title "ecumenical bishop" in order to emphasize the authority of the patriarchs. Gregory denounced such titles as sins of vanity and pride. Such was his purity and conviction that he objected on the same grounds when the bishop of Alexandria referred to Gregory himself as "Universal Pope." He preferred to be known as the "servant of the servants of God."

Expanding efforts. Through the years, some bishops had used their positions to gain wealth and status. Some were appointed as rewards for favors they had done for more powerful politicians. Gregory, however, felt he was responsible for the care of the church as a whole and made it his responsibility to make sure that elected bishops were following procedures prescribed by the church. As his own power grew, he appointed the governors of Italian cities, intervening in civil government. Concerned with the lay control of the independent Frankish Church, he installed a representative for the people of France and suggested a plan for reform. The pope's continued efforts allowed for later reunification of the Frankish Church and the church in Rome.

Gregory's missionary vision was not limited to Italy; he wrote to other bishops in Spain, Gaul, and Africa, used monks as ambassadors and emissaries, and promoted the conversion of the Visigoths and Germanic tribes. In 597 he sent forty monks, led by Augustine of Canterbury, to Great Britain. Augustine and his missionaries secured England's loyalty to the papacy and Christianity.

Writings. Books were another way of spreading the faith. Gregory balanced abstract ideals with the practical needs of medieval Christianity. His writing simplified and clarified the complicated church doctrines. Uneducated and less cultured people could then hear and understand the ideas of their own religion. His *Dialogues on the Life and Miracles of the Saints and on*

▶

Gregory the Great sending forty monks, including Augustine of Canterbury, to Great Britain to secure England's loyalty to the papacy.

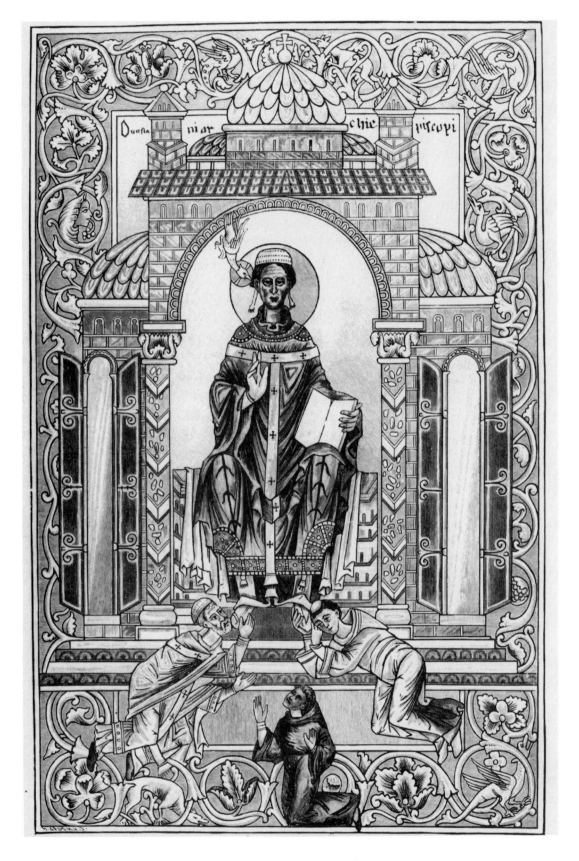

the Immortality of Souls, written in 594, is a series of conversations between himself and the Roman archdeacon Peter. The first three books describe the holy lives in fantastic tales of visions, dreams, and miraculous powers; the fourth book presents Gregory's own understanding of theology.

Purgatory. In his writing, Gregory focuses on themes of sin, judgment, and atonement (penance). His explanations drew on the thoughts of earlier church leaders, particularly St. Augustine of Hippo (354-430). The idea of a "second repentance" for sins not forgiven in this life was not original; however, he is the main source of teachings about purgatory. The faithful, Gregory taught, enter heaven immediately after death; purgatory exists for those who are yet unprepared to meet God. Participating in the rite of the Mass, said Gregory, can help speed the souls through. This idea of purgatory extended the need for the church into the future, and the idea became a central doctrine in the centuries to follow.

The Power of Pope Gregory

While expanding the church in Africa and England, Gregory built the power of the pope in Italy. He "ordered the police, regulated markets, coined money, maintained civil and criminal courts, repaired the walls and aqueducts [of Rome], supported schools and hospitals, commanded the militia, and defended the city in the case of attack." (Thompson, p. 132)

Pastoral Rule. Gregory's most influential text, his guide for bishops, became the standard manual for church leaders by the ninth century. This volume, *The Book of Pastoral Rule,* made the monk Benedict of Nursia the model of devotion. The book outlines proper conduct, personality, and attitude toward teaching, and warns of the temptations accompanying power. Clergy must be celibate, live with compassion and meditation, be good speakers, and teach through example and illustration.

Worship. Gregory's name translates to "preacher of the flock." He published twenty-two sermons on Ezekiel and forty sermons on the gospel that blend vivid images with words of comfort. He is credited with creating the offices, or hours of prayer, and the "plainsong" now known as Gregorian chant. He simplified the litany into a sung prayer in which the clergy and the congregation sang alternate phrases.

Aftermath

Preserving Christianity. Gregory the Great can be seen as a bridge between the wisdom of the ancient church and the Latin West, enabling it to survive and even flourish in the new world of the following centuries. He shaped the institutions and the life of the Roman church in ways that are still felt today. He was able to establish foreign contact, command military might, minister to the poor, and provide organization to the scattered church. Because it was the pope who administered these duties, rather than the civil forces, the papacy remained the ruling force in Italy for several centuries.

In his last days, Gregory was so ill that he could hardly get out of bed long enough to preside over the holy sacrifice on the church's great feast day. He died March 12, 604, leaving behind writings that would be translated into English and used as guides to Christian life centuries later. His letters were published in a book simply called *Letters,* and these remain today's best view of a dedicated and capable church leader.

Little over a hundred years later, the Franks would use the strong church organization established by Gregory to build an empire sanctified by the popes.

For More Information

Clouse, Robert G. *Gregory the Great and the Medieval Church: Great Leaders of the Christian Church.* Edited by John D. Woodbridge. Chicago: Moody Press, 1988.

de Voragine, Jacobus. *The Golden Legend.* Printed 1298. Translated from the Latin by Ryan Granger and Helmut Ripperger, 1850. Reprint, New York: Arno Press, 1969.

Lampe, G. W. H., editor. *The Cambridge History of the Bible.* Vol. 2. New York: Cambridge University Press, 1969.

Thompson, J. W. *Economic and Social History of the Middle Ages.* New York: Century, 1928.

Walker, Williston, and Richard A. Norris, editors. *A History of the Christian Church.* New York: Charles Scribner's Sons, 1985.

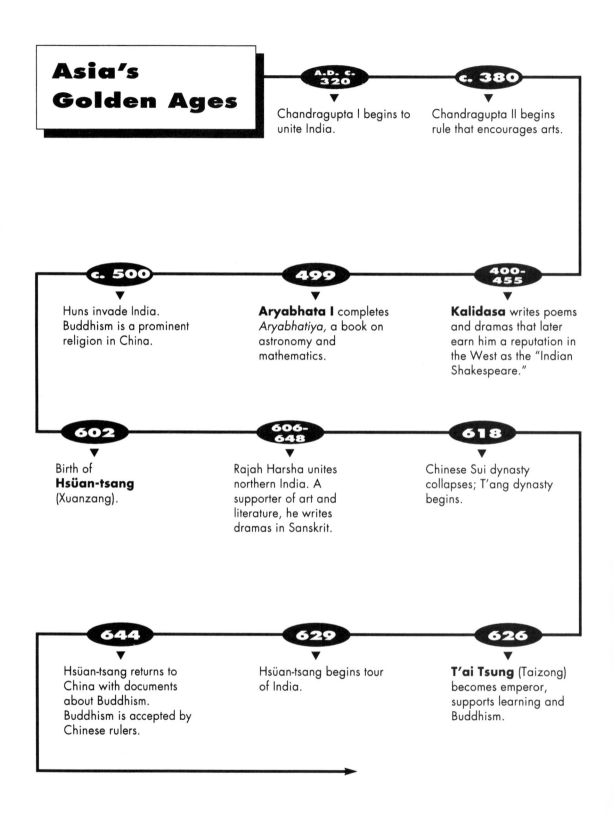

Asia's Golden Ages

A.D. c. 320
Chandragupta I begins to unite India.

c. 380
Chandragupta II begins rule that encourages arts.

c. 500
Huns invade India. Buddhism is a prominent religion in China.

499
Aryabhata I completes *Aryabhatiya*, a book on astronomy and mathematics.

400-455
Kalidasa writes poems and dramas that later earn him a reputation in the West as the "Indian Shakespeare."

602
Birth of **Hsüan-tsang** (Xuanzang).

606-648
Rajah Harsha unites northern India. A supporter of art and literature, he writes dramas in Sanskrit.

618
Chinese Sui dynasty collapses; T'ang dynasty begins.

644
Hsüan-tsang returns to China with documents about Buddhism. Buddhism is accepted by Chinese rulers.

629
Hsüan-tsang begins tour of India.

626
T'ai Tsung (Taizong) becomes emperor, supports learning and Buddhism.

ASIA'S
GOLDEN AGES

Between A.D. 300 and 900, two great dynasties rose and fell, one in China and the other in India. The Gupta dynasty in India and the later T'ang dynasty of China brought periods of peace, good government, and prosperity to their countries. And in either nation, long-standing religious traditions became unifying forces as well. Nearly one thousand years earlier, Buddhism had arisen and become established in India in reaction to Hinduism, an aged religion that had become laden with ritual and ceremony. But during the Gupta dynasty, a revised form of Hinduism became a strong force and nearly drove Buddhism out of India. By that time, however, Buddhism had spread eastward and swept through China, where it became established as the primary religion of the Chinese people. In both India and China during Asia's golden ages, these two great eastern religions were supported by kindly, scholarly rulers who encouraged art, literature, science, and medicine.

The greatest achievements in science, medicine, and mathematics developed in India. Astronomers studied the heavens and developed sophisticated methods for measuring the paths of planets and moons. In the process, mathematics was greatly simplified by the invention first of alphabetical symbols for numerals and later of the current number system, referred to as Arabic numerals.

Other Indian mathematicians developed the decimal system. The most famous of the astronomers/mathematicians may have been **Aryabhata I.** The ideas of measurement and of geometry, which were collected in his book *Aryabhatiya,* were carried into the Middle East and eventually served as the foundations of Western mathematics. At the same time, Indian scholars were making important discoveries in chemistry and medicine. Indian, and later Chinese, doctors began studies and descriptions of diseases, along with detailed accounts of herbal remedies.

Literature in the old but exact Sanskrit language of India was revived and added to—a collection of folktales was expanded between A.D. 300 and 500, later to be published as the *Panchatantra.* One of the greatest Indian authors was the poet and dramatist **Kalidasa** of the Gupta era. His dramas later brought him renown in the West, where he is sometimes referred to as the "Indian Shakespeare," although in point of time William Shakespeare should rightly be the "English Kalidasa."

Trade between the two great Eastern powers expanded during this period. However, India, weakened by the costs of defending against such invaders as the Huns, who began raiding northern India about 500, let support of the arts and sciences lapse for a short time. Then two great events of the early seventh century reignited Indian scholarship so that it thrived in the region until the coming of Europeans in the fifteenth century. The reuniting of India under Rajah Harsha, a strong leader who supported the arts, gave rise to a new wave of Indian literature. Then the famous walk around India by **Hsüan-tsang** (also spelled Xuanzang) resulted not only in increased trade between the powers but also in exchanges of ideas about religion, sciences, mathematics, and the arts.

Hsüan-tsang was a Chinese Buddhist monk and scholar who, lamenting the scarcity of Buddhist writings in his own language, vowed to learn the Indian language Sanskrit and bring the full message of Buddhism to China. He began his eleven-year walk around India in 629, during the reign of the second emperor of the T'ang dynasty, **T'ai Tsung** (or Taizong). This ruler's encouragement of the arts and sciences gave rise to the "golden age" of China.

During T'ai Tsung's reign and those of the T'ang rulers to follow, China renewed its interest in practical applications of science. Chinese chemists added greatly to the knowledge of textiles and dyes. Chinese inventors developed block printing and experimented with different types of inks. They also are credited with the creation of navigational and surveying tools such as the compass. Encouraged by the philosophy of Confucius, which was nearly a religion of the aristocracy, learning became a requirement for positions in civil service. Mastery of the complex writing system of Chinese became essential and education in it universally available. Its dependence on delicate brush strokes led to similarly simple and delicate styles in art. Schools of art opened everywhere, and artists such as Wu Tao-tzu (also spelled Wu Tao-hsüan or Wu Daoxuan, c. 700-760) began to develop the styles that pervade present-day Chinese art. In this period, the artistry of the great terra cotta figurines identified with China reached their heights, as did the technology for producing porcelain.

Poetry had long been a passion with the people of Asia. Aryabhata, in fact, had written his book about Indian mathematics and astronomy in poetical verse. In China two of the world's greatest poets appeared about the same time and encouraged each other through their writing. Li T'ai-po (or Li Bai) and Tu Fu (or Du Fu) both wrote in the eighth century, and scholars still debate which one was China's greatest poet. Li T'ai-po and Tu Fu often exchanged barbs in poetical form. Tu Fu gently chided Li T'ai-po for heavy drinking, while Li T'ai-po accused Tu Fu of being too involved with his work, "suffering from poetry again." These two may have been the best in an age that produced poetry that was pruned in the 1700s into an anthology of 48,900 poems by 2,300 poets.

All of these cultural advances swept across Asia through Indian and Chinese expansions, and much later influenced Western philosophy, science, and the arts. Indian ideas pervaded the cultural, religious, and political climate of Southeast Asia, while China's ideas were carried to Korea and the Pacific Islands, including Japan. Beginning with these expansions, Indian and Chinese influences in philosophy, science, and the arts were spread throughout the world.

Kalidasa

c. 400-455

Personal Background

Kalidasa was most likely born about A.D. 400, but the date of his birth, however, is in question. Sometimes it is estimated to be near 100 B.C. and at other times, A.D. 600. What we know of Kalidasa has been gathered mostly from his writings, but part of the confusion regarding his birth date is that Kalidasa served in the court of a king named Vikramaditya. Unfortunately, this name, which means "Son of Valor," was taken by several Indian kings of different eras. One of these was Chandragupta II. The contents of Kalidasa's writing and world history hint that he was born in Ujjain, the capital city of India under the rule of Chandragupta II.

Early life. Popular legends claim that Kalidasa was an orphan slave who was eventually freed because he impressed his master with his intelligence. Today's students of Indian history believe that this view is not quite true. More likely, Kalidasa grew up with plenty of money and privileges at a time when India, and especially the capital city, were very prosperous. India was then ruled by the skillful Gupta family, and according to modern scholars, Kalidasa lived in an aristocratic society, characterized by material luxury, fine aesthetic tastes, polite culture, and appreciation of art and learning. It is also probable that Kalidasa was a member of the royal court. Such an atmosphere might have stimulated his mind and encouraged him to express himself.

▲ An 18th-century Indo-Persian miniature of the princess Shakuntala, heroine of one of Kalidasa's plays.

Event: Developing Indian literature.

Role: Writing in the golden age of Indian literature and science, Kalidasa became the most famous of ancient Indian writers. His poems and plays, based on legends about Indian gods, the beauty of nature, and human desires, raised Indian literature to new heights of achievement.

The Guptas and the golden age of India. It is likely that Kalidasa was a member of the court of Chandragupta II, who ruled India from about A.D. 380 to 415. About 388 Chandragupta defeated the Sakas, neighboring enemies, giving India some protection from foreign threats and assurance of self-government. For centuries before and after the Guptas, India was governed by foreign leaders. In the brief Gupta period of self-government India thrived. Ujjain became the most brilliant capital of the world, and Chandragupta an avid supporter of the arts and sciences.

Gems of the court. During his reign, Chandragupta II assembled a group of nine outstanding scientists and poets, including Kalidasa, who came to be known as the gems of Chandragupta's court. Knowledge became India's most prized possession during this golden age. In fact, it was the mathematicians in the Gupta period who invented the decimal system and Arabic numerals, still in use today.

Gupta Literature and Religion

Writings during the Gupta dynasty were heavily intertwined with religion. The most popular religion in India was Hinduism, a faith that has an array of gods, in addition to a holy trinity: Brahma, the creator, Vishnu, the preserver, and Shiva, the destroyer. Kalidasa dedicated all his writings to Shiva, the patron god of literature.

Kalidasa's interests and inspirations. From his own writing, it appears that Kalidasa was most interested in beauty—beauty in nature and beauty in women. His interest in the beauty of nature may have led him to travel throughout India and write his long poem, *The Dynasty of Raghu,* that tells of the beauty of the land. Nearly all of his writings concern beautiful women and romance. In *The Meghaduta,* another of his long poems, he describes the loveliness of a woman:

> In the syama vine I see thy body;
>   in the eye of the startled doe, thy glance;
> In the moon, the sheen of thy cheek;
>   in the peacock's massive plumes, thy hair;
> In the delicate river-ripples I descry the play of thine eyebrows;
> Nowhere, alas, O gentle one, is thy likeness found in a single
>   place.

(from verse 100, as translated in Dimock, p. 123)

Because of the romantic themes in his writings, historians have suggested that Kalidasa was, perhaps, handsome and charming, which resulted in women being as interested in him as much as he was interested in them.

The writers of Kalidasa's day frequently wove religion into their works, and his was no different from the others. The mysticism and art of the Hindu religion interested him to some extent, but Kalidasa was probably far more interested in conditions of this life than in spiritual matters. Most of his work concerns common life subjects, about which he wrote in amusing and refreshing styles and with a lightheartedness that shines through his work. Certainly his writing reveals a very positive personality. He seemed to appreciate all that life had to offer him, from affairs of high society to the peacefulness of nature.

Participation: Developing Indian Literature

Sanskrit language. Invasion and foreign control have played an important role in Indian language. Somewhere between three thousand and two thousand years ago, Indo-Europeans from central Asia invaded the land, bringing with them an oral language, Sanskrit. The earliest Indian literature was recited orally in that language, though it was not written until long after the spoken forms became popular. At the time of Buddha, in about 500 B.C., a revised, "pure" form of Sanskrit was the language of the ruling classes. It was not, however, for another two hundred years or more that Sanskrit in India became a written language. By that time Buddhists had begun to use several different Indian dialects related to Sanskrit called Prakrits.

Kalidasa on the Soul

Kalidasa believed that the only real thing in the universe is the soul and that everything else is illusion. According to this view, the soul is made up of three parts: *sattva*, "true quantities"; *rajas*, "passionate frailties"; and *tamas*, "dark qualities." Every soul is thought to have a different combination of these three components, making the possessor of the soul more or less passionate, true, or dark.

Sanskrit literature. The Greeks under Alexander the Great (356-323 B.C.) had invaded northern India before the Gupta period, but there is no sign that Greek drama influenced Indian literature. In fact, there seems to be no foreign influence on the

Indian literature of this period. Still, Greek, Indian, and English literature share common threads—themes about gods and royalty, refined and poetic language, and strong moral messages. Indian literature, like the others, was based mostly on the myths, legends, and rituals of its own culture. Only a few writers, one of them Kalidasa, attempted to invent themes of their own.

Kalidasa and other writers were expected to follow the strict and complicated writing rules published in the *Natyashastra,* the book of Indian dance, music, and drama. The book was written by Bharata, a wise man of India, and was published about two hundred years before Kalidasa began his writing. One of Bharata's requirements was that an author was supposed to use all the different forms of Sanskrit in one play; pure Sanskrit might be used by the royal characters and a Prakrit dialect for the peasants. Another rule was that a play could not be a tragedy, as there should be no death on stage. Each play was to begin and end with a prayer, and each play was supposed to include eight basic human feelings: desire, comic joy, anger, sadness, pride, fear, loathing, and wonder. To accomplish all these prescriptions, Indian Sanskrit plays took many forms, some of them containing as many as ten acts, and Indian poems were also carried to great lengths.

Indian Theater Sets

In Indian theater of Kalidasa's era, there were few or preferably no stage props, not even a curtain in front. The stage itself was quite simple, just a raised platform with a pillar at each corner. A curtain in the rear was split at center stage. Actors came on stage through this split.

The rear curtain and the costumes were important to the play. A curtain gently held apart by two beautiful attendants indicated a solemn entrance and scene. An actor in a violent scene might indicate his fierce emotion by leaping through the curtain, tearing it open himself. Different colored costumes indicated different moods. Red, for example, indicated a violent character; white, sensuality.

Performing. Both Sanskrit plays and poems were designed to be acted out. A poem was meant to be recited in front of an audience, often by the author himself. Kalidasa probably read his own poems to the court and perhaps introduced his plays personally while the players were preparing to present them.

Powerful words. Sanskrit dramas depended heavily on dialogue. There was little action on stage, except that the actor was supposed to mime well enough to make props unnecessary. But the words of Kalidasa told the story of the play. The word-pictures he provided were outstanding, making him one of the great playwrights of history. He has been called the "Indian Shakespeare," in reference to the popular English dramatist and poet. Even when translated into another language, a very difficult task because of the complexity of Sanskrit, Kalidasa's words are poetic and interesting.

One of Kalidasa's most famous plays is *Shakuntala*. In the drama a king falls in love with the maiden Shakuntala and gives her a ring in marriage. The king is then called away to the capital and leaves the now pregnant Shakuntala behind. Meanwhile, an angry hermit visits Shakuntala and curses her, saying that her husband will forget who she is until he sees her wedding ring. Desiring to win back her husband and the father of her child, Shakuntala travels to the capital in the company of three hermits. They bring a message from Shakuntala's father, who had been absent during the wedding, that he finally approves the union. After a number of distractions, including a war, Shakuntala is reunited with the king, who is proud of his young son Bharata.

Aftermath

The legacy of Kalidasa. Kalidasa's great ability was acknowledged by his contemporaries, and he contributed greatly to the development of Indian literature. Through the patronage of Chandragupta II, he and other great writers, scientists, and philosophers took India into a golden age. Kalidasa's works continue to provide insight into the culture of ancient India and serve as examples of literary excellence for Indian culture even today.

For More Information

Basham, A. L. *The Wonder That Was India.* New York: Hawthorne, 1963.

Dimock, Edward C. *The Literatures of India.* Chicago: University of Chicago Press, 1974.

Gargi, Balwant. *Theater in India.* New York: Theater Arts, 1962.

Lal, P. *Great Sanskrit Plays in Modern Translation.* New York: New Directions, 1964.

Sheykhar, Indu. *Sanskrit Drama: Its Origin and Decline.* Leiden, The Netherlands: E. J. Brill, 1960.

T'ai Tsung

600-649

Personal Background

Early life. Toward the end of the sixth century A.D., China was ruled by a dynasty that survived only two rulers. It was just as the second of these rulers was coming into power that a son was born to Li Yuan, the prince of T'ang, in a Chinese province in the northeast. Born in 597, Li Yuan's son Li Shih-min would someday make both father and son famous and would later adopt the name T'ai Tsung (also spelled Taizong). Li Shih-min had two brothers and at least one sister, and his father was a wise and honest man who taught his children the sayings of Confucius and raised them to respect his teachings. That was to be expected, since the aristocrats of China followed Confucius, even though most of the Chinese were rapidly taking up Buddhism.

Life on the Chinese border. Li Yuan was the governor of a district that was on the Chinese frontier. He managed to keep his district under Chinese control and its people among the most prosperous and happy of all the people of China, even though they were constantly threatened by northern tribes, particularly the Turks. As Li Shih-min grew up, he learned to defend himself against the Turkish nomads and Chinese outlaws who frequently raided his father's border regions. Consequently, he fought many battles as a teenager alongside his father and learned early on many things that would help him to be a great emperor one day.

▲ A T'ang-era print of Confucius; T'ai Tsung's attitude as well as his governmental policies were shaped by traditional Confucian values.

Event: Preserving Confucian ideas.

Role: T'ai Tsung was the second emperor of the T'ang dynasty in China. With his extraordinary courage and wisdom, he unified and expanded the Chinese Empire. His tolerant attitude toward foreign ideas and his desire to improve Chinese society helped to create China's golden age.

Tradition and the Sui. Chinese tradition held that a man devoted to the good of his people would come to reign over them so lightly that they would not even know they were being governed. That ruler would start a family dynasty but, after a while, one member of the dynasty would turn out to be a cruel and unwise ruler. That leader would soon be replaced by a wise ruler from another family, beginning a new dynasty.

Although the Sui dynasty had begun only in 582, it was already, according to tradition, becoming corrupt when Li Shih-min became an adult. In fact, there were so many hardships affecting China—civil wars, raids by northern tribes, and corruption in local governments—that the young man dreamed of earlier and happier days when all of China lived without fear of the raiders to the north, without fear of hunger, or without fighting among themselves. Li Yuan's district was one of the few where the people lived free of poverty and of government corruption. It is said that the contrast between Li Shih-min's home district and other parts of China was the reason Li Shih-min decided to take action.

Participation: A Golden Age in China

Li Shih-min's plan. The young Li Shih-min grew impatient with what he believed to be a bad Sui government. He was certain that his father would be a better ruler of China, but Li Yuan remained loyal to the Sui emperor Yang Kuang (also known as Yang Ti [Yangdi], "zealous emperor"). Li Shih-min begged his father to gather an army and drive out the emperor, but he refused. Li Shih-min, however, had become an extremely cunning and brave young man. When he was only about twenty years old, he devised a plan that would force his father to act and re-establish order in China.

According to legend, Li Shih-min befriended one of the eunuchs (castrated men) in charge of the emperor's harem. He convinced the eunuch to introduce Li Yuan to a particularly attractive young woman, who was to become part of the emperor's harem. Unaware of this, Li Yuan made the mistake of making love with her.

Having a love affair with a member of the emperor's harem was against the law. Upon realizing this, Li Yuan, now an outlaw, began to gather an army to protect himself. Though he said he was gearing up to protect the emperor from his opponents, Li Yuan, with his army of thirty thousand, planned to take the throne. Li Shih-min's sister, according to another legend, use her wealth to recruit another army to help. Her army of ten thousand attracted other recruits and won a pledge of help from their former enemies, the Turks.

After a short time, Li Shih-min and his father had gathered about sixty thousand soldiers who, as Li Yuan had claimed, were used legitimately to conquer the illegal governments that had formed in the Chinese provinces. Li Shih-min personally rode out on horseback to command the army that had formed. Though he was almost killed in the first battle, he did not stop. Meanwhile, the capital city of Siking (present-day Sian or Changan) was in a state of confusion. Yang Kuang tried to escape, but palace guards assassinated the Sui emperor in 618.

The beginning of the T'ang dynasty. Upon hearing that the emperor was dead, Li Yuan declared himself the military commander of China. A few months later, Li Shih-min persuaded his father to declare himself emperor, because there was no Sui heir to the throne. But the strife in China continued and many governors questioned Li Yuan's right to govern. The first task was to reunite China. That job fell to the commander of the rebel army, Li Shih-min.

For the following four years, as Li Shih-min fought to restore order in the Chinese Empire, he became a famous and respected warrior. He was so admired that his two brothers, and even his father, grew jealous of him. Both of his brothers were treacherous, and they began to worry that Li Shih-min would someday become emperor, even though the older one was the crowned prince and future emperor.

Chinese Emperors and Their Harems

Chinese emperors often kept very large harems to entertain them in their great palaces. The women, and the eunuchs who guarded them, had sometimes been a source of revolution from within the palace walls. T'ai Tsung had used a palace woman to trick his father and knew of their potential to make trouble. Shortly after T'ai Tsung took office as the emperor, he expelled more than three thousand women from the palace.

The plot to kill Li Shih-min. Once peace was restored to the empire, Li Shih-min returned to live in the imperial palace and his brothers began plotting to have him killed. First they tried to poison him at a banquet they held in his honor, but Li Shih-min took an antidote and recovered.

Next they hired assassins to hide near the palace gates to shoot Li Shih-min with arrows when he approached. However, a traitor involved in the plot gave warning about the ambush. As Li Shih-min rode up to the palace in darkness, his would-be assassins shot many arrows but missed him. Li Shih-min, however, shot and killed one of his brothers on his first attempt and his other brother was killed by a lieutenant.

When Li Yuan heard of what had happened, he was very angry at Li Shih-min. He knew, however, that his two sons had resorted to treachery in the past and, once the emperor's advisers reminded him of Li Shih-min's superior morals, he decided to forgive the killings.

Li Shih-min becomes Emperor T'ai Tsung. In 626 Li Yuan praised his remaining son for saving the family's reputation and offered him the throne. Twice the heroic general refused to accept it. Finally he was ordered by Li Yuan to become emperor. He could not refuse an order, and so he finally accepted the throne, taking the name T'ai Tsung, "grand ancestor." One of the first orders he gave was to have his sisters-in-law and his nephews killed, to protect himself from their revenge.

The very same month that he became emperor, T'ai Tsung faced invasion by the Turkish nomads from the west. They marched into the capital and threatened to take over the empire unless the emperor paid them. Against the wishes of the imperial advisers, T'ai Tsung challenged them, though he did not have a large enough army to win. He rode out on a great white stallion to inform the Turks that his people were prepared to fight, but he could not understand why the Turks would now break the alliance that had defeated Yang Kuang. T'ai Tsung had built such a reputation in his previous years of battle that the Turks feared him. At the sight of the emperor on his stallion they backed down and agreed to abide by the former treaty. This was the last time that the Turks attempted to invade China.

After he had driven out the Turkish nomads, T'ai Tsung continued to use his military reputation to secure and expand the Chinese Empire. Within twenty years, the empire's boundaries reached to the borders of India and Persia. This period of Chinese glory lasted for 137 years and is known as China's golden age.

Confucianist philosophy and tolerance. T'ai Tsung was a man of remarkable character with strong affection for his people. Though he was the emperor, he accepted the advice of others. When the Buddhist monk and scholar **Hsüan-tsang** (see entry) returned from his pilgrimage to India, for instance, T'ai Tsung met with him and discussed religion with him. In fact, after talking with Hsüan-tsang, T'ai Tsung eventually converted to Buddhism.

However, T'ai Tsung always believed that Confucianist philosophy was the best by which to govern the empire. Confucius had said that if sons knew their place and respected their parents, and if parents knew their place and respected local officials, and if that respect and caring reached all the way to the emperor, then the nation would live in peace, prosperity, and freedom from fear. Although Buddhism was the most popular religion of his time, T'ai Tsung chose Confucianists as his advisers. He believed, as Confucius had, that the emperor was to rule for the people, not for himself. "The first principle in kingship is to preserve the people," T'ai Tsung once said. "A king who exploits the people for his personal gains is like a man who cuts his own thighs to feed himself" (Li, p. 170). T'ai Tsung gained the respect of everyone he came in contact with.

> ## T'ai Tsung the Showman
>
> T'ai Tsung made an example of the military leaders who had attempted to take over the empire. He returned to the capital city of Siking victorious in 621, riding on horseback while the captured pretenders to the throne were on foot on either side of him.

Legendary changes. Where China had once been chaotic and, in some places, lawless, it had now become a most respectable society. Legend claims that T'ai Tsung once freed more than three hundred convicted criminals who were sentenced to death so they could live their final days with their families—as long as they agreed to return to prison at least one day before their execution. The legend claims that all of them returned.

Under T'ai Tsung's rule the cities had become almost crime-free, and taxes were at their lowest rate in China's history. Unlike the emperors before him, T'ai Tsung was very devoted to his country, and he was smart enough and strong enough to maintain order while also protecting the empire from invasion.

China's culture grows. With a strong and respected government, China flourished. T'ai Tsung organized the empire and promoted public education. For the first time in history, China was divided into legal provinces, and the government began to take a census. The census was necessary because the emperor planned to rid the land of wealthy landowners. Each Chinese peasant was to receive about thirteen and one-half acres to farm. It was a plan to make all Chinese more free, but it also made it possible for them to pay their taxes.

The emperor used these taxes to improve education and support art and literature. T'ai Tsung had schools and colleges built to educate the population and train people for government service. The schools were not free, but the cost was so low that nearly everyone could afford to have a good education. This education focused on a knowledge of the books assembled by Confucius. T'ai Tsung used these books to strengthen the examination system that selected government officials. In T'ai Tsung's system, even the poorest peasant, no matter how old or young, could hope to become a high-level government official—even, perhaps, the emperor.

T'ai Tsung also had libraries built and had his learned men gather information from every known country. The imperial palace became a gathering place for the intellectuals of China. He established new trade with nations such as Persia and India, and not only did China's economy become healthy once again, but many new ideas about science and art were also traded along with goods. The Chinese used the imported ideas to improve their methods of writing, sculpting, painting, and making calendars and medicine, among other things. In exchange, Chinese inventions such as paper and printing spread to the Near East and West. T'ai Tsung had transformed China from a disorganized, struggling society to the world's most glorious empire of its time. The culture that was built during T'ai Tsung's rule has remained a source of pride and enrichment for the Chinese today.

Religious tolerance. Religious diversity was another outcome of the new Chinese openness. T'ai Tsung's government already accepted Buddhism and Confucianism. Under his rule, a group of Christians found acceptance in China, as did such Middle Eastern religions as Zoroastrianism.

Aftermath

A warrior's death. When T'ai Tsung died in 649, he was buried in a tomb decorated to illustrate his greatest glories. As was the custom with many ancient leaders, the emperor had prepared his own burial place. Placed inside the tomb he had statues of kings he had conquered, and on the walls he had carved images of favorite horses he had ridden in battle. He had fought harder than anyone else to advance Chinese civilization, and he was very proud of his victories.

The legacy of T'ai Tsung. T'ai Tsung's twenty-two-year-old son Li Chih (reign title Kao Tsung, or Gaozong) became emperor in 650. He was not as gifted a ruler as T'ai Tsung, in his later years being greatly influenced by his consort, the empress Wu. For the next century, China remained peaceful and prosperous. The foundation that T'ai Tsung had laid, which started with a clever plot, served to provide China with one of its most wonderful eras. The T'ang dynasty lasted until 907 and was followed by the Song dynasty some years later. The life of T'ai Tsung served as an example for all statesmen who succeeded him, and his love for education, literature, and art ensured that the reign of the T'ang dynasty would be forever remembered as the golden age of China.

For More Information

Goodrich, L. Carrington. *A Short History of the Chinese People.* New York: Harper and Brothers, 1959.

Hookham, Hilda. *A Short History of China.* New York: St. Martin's, 1970.

Li, Dun J. *The Ageless Chinese: A History.* New York: Charles Scribner's Sons, 1978.

Seeger, Elizabeth. *The Pageant of Chinese History.* New York: David McKay, 1962.

Hsüan-tsang

602-664

Personal Background

Early life. Hsüan-tsang (or Xuanzang) was born in 602 in Henan, China. His father was a government official and wise man who raised Hsüan-tsang in the tradition of Confucian philosophy, which taught that each citizen should find his place in society and keep it. Hsüan-tsang was a very intelligent, organized, and determined young man who seemed capable of doing anything that he put his mind to. The one thing that Hsüan-tsang wanted more than anything else was to become more religious.

For several hundred years, the Chinese rulers had favored the ideas of Confucius, but by the first century A.D., a more flexible religion came to China from India. This religion, Buddhism, allowed the Chinese people to include some of their old beliefs and god figures. Easy to adjust to, Buddhism soon swept across China. As a young man, Hsüan-tsang had changed his religion from Confucianism to Buddhism. And, wanting to be like the Buddhists who gave their lives to their religion, he soon became a monk. With his sharp mind and an unusually strong devotion to his faith, he quickly became a respected teacher of Buddhism.

Believer in a foreign faith. Confucianism and Taoism were the two most popular native Chinese religions. Buddhism was also popular, but it had originated in India, and all of the sacred Buddhist texts were written in Indian languages such as Sanskrit

▲ A T'ang-era figure of seated Buddha; Hsüan-tsang, wanting to be like the Buddhists who gave their lives to their religion, became a monk.

Event: Bringing Buddhist literature to China.

Role: Hsüan-tsang was a Chinese Buddhist teacher and scholar who made an historic pilgrimage to India, where he spent fifteen years learning the Sanskrit language, receiving Buddhist training, visiting holy places, and documenting Indian culture. When he returned to China, he made this information available to the Chinese people, helping to spread Buddhism in China and bringing new ideas to its people.

or Pali. Because no one in China was able to translate from Sanskrit to Chinese very well, the Buddhist texts that were available in China were incomplete or unclear.

Hsüan-tsang was not satisfied teaching from the poorly translated Buddhist texts, which prompted arguments within the Chinese Buddhist community because the translations were unclear. He was determined to go to India, learn the complicated Sanskrit language, and translate the sacred texts. Travel from China to India by Chinese Buddhists was not a new idea. As early as 399, Fa-hsien (also spelled Faxian) had traveled the Tarim River basin into India and returned to China by sea. Other Buddhists had followed over the years. Still, Hsüan-tsang's decision was a difficult one, for a trip from China to India in his day was extremely dangerous.

The reign of T'ai Tsung. Following the overthrow of the Sui dynasty, China was in a state of chaos and civil war. Various groups fought to control the Chinese territory and its government. In 627 an emperor came forward, **T'ai Tsung** (or Taizong; see entry), who began to turn the chaos into order.

Buddhism in China

The first reported Buddhist community in China was started between A.D. 60 and 70. By the year 500 Buddhism had become widely popular and deeply rooted in the culture of China. It appealed most to the urban class.

T'ai Tsung established T'ang rule in China one province at a time while also fighting off an invasion by the Turks. One by one, he brought the other kingdoms in China under T'ang control. Ruling from 627 to 650, he and his government would eventually establish a basis for a century of peace and prosperity. However, at the time that Hsüan-tsang was thinking about Buddhism and India, the T'ang dynasty was involved in a civil war.

Participation: Pilgrimage to India

An incredible journey. Chinese outlaws and enemy soldiers took advantage of the government's problems to roam the frontier border between China, Persia, and India. Perhaps because of such dangers, the government forbade Chinese citizens to travel into or past the Chinese frontier to the west. Therefore, when Hsüan-tsang asked for permission to travel to India, he was refused.

Hsüan-tsang, however, was determined to visit India, the Buddhist holy land. He did not have a passport and so was forced to travel in secrecy without a guide. He set out in September 629 from Siking (present-day Sian or Changan) in northwestern China to walk to India. The journey took Hsüan-tsang through desert and the Himalaya mountains, through a bit of Persia, and then south into India—a distance of nearly 1,700 miles. The climate of the Gobi Desert, in the early part of the journey, was particularly inhospitable, and he nearly died. Perhaps Hsüan-tsang's uncommon faith in Buddha gave him the courage to go on with his journey.

Hsüan-tsang's diary. Throughout his travels, Hsüan-tsang kept a detailed diary of all he encountered. He wrote about the landscape of areas such as the Chinese frontier and the approaches of Persia, which had not yet been charted by the Chinese. Through these records, it is apparent that Hsüan-tsang was an excellent explorer and geographer, and that is how he managed to make the pilgrimage without a guide.

Hsüan-tsang also wrote about the peoples he met, describing their languages, institutions, customs, superstitions, religions, philosophies, and agricultural and commercial activities. He met political leaders and wrote about their policies and practices, information that later became valuable to the emperor of China in making political decisions.

When Hsüan-tsang finally arrived in India sometime in 630, he was received with warmth and curiosity. His fellow Buddhists were very excited to meet him, as word had traveled about his dangerous pilgrimage to get to the holy land. Indian nobles were curious to meet the crazy Chinese man who had traveled illegally and risked his life to come to India.

In India. The Gupta dynasty in India had reached its peak in the reign of Chandragupta II, who had died in 413. From that time on, India had been plagued with invasions led by Huns, civil wars among small governments along the Ganges River, and violent, lying kings with little regard for their subjects or religion. Finally, a strong leader emerged. Between 606 and 612, Rajah Harsha reunited nearly all of India. He was the ruler when Hsüan-tsang arrived in India. The Chinese monk found a well-established caste system and a secure and thoughtful government that managed to keep taxes low while maintaining a high standard of living. Above all, Hsüan-tsang found a government that had a high respect for learning. Harsha was a skillful politician, soldier, poet, dramatist, and champion of the arts. Hsüan-tsang recorded his observations, giving modern students one of the few real looks at this period in India.

Visiting the holy land. While in India, Hsüan-tsang traveled along the entire perimeter of the empire; though it was not as long then as is today's nine-thousand-mile trip, it was still a lengthy journey. He learned the Sanskrit language, which had a complicated structure that made it difficult to translate into other languages. He was trained in the traditional ways of Buddhism by Indian holy men, and he visited the holy places of the original Buddha's life and death.

The famous pilgrim's homecoming. Although Hsüan-tsang had left China illegally, he was given a fine welcome when he returned in 644. People of all levels of society came for his official welcome home. Buddhist monks and nuns, scholars, imperial and local officials, and the citizens of the capital city of Siking lined the road to the Hong Fu Monastery to greet Hsüan-tsang. Many people burned incense and scattered flowers in celebration of Hsüan-tsang's historic journey.

The emperor T'ai Tsung and his government were pleased to see him, because he had collected valuable information in the areas of philosophy, science, art, and the political policies of India. T'ai Tsung granted a personal interview to Hsüan-tsang and even asked him to become an imperial adviser. Hsüan-tsang chose not to do so, preferring instead to remain a monk. However, information from Hsüan-tsang and other Chinese travelers became very useful to the emperor. It helped him to plan political strategies and strengthen the Chinese empire.

Of course, the Chinese Buddhists were delighted to have him home as well. They now had answers to their questions about Buddha and the religion that he had inspired. Through the incredible journey he had completed, the detailed diary he had kept, and the items he had brought home with him, Hsüan-tsang

▲ The Sanskrit Buddhist work *Vajracchedikā prajňa pāramitā* in Chinese translation, printed in 868 and found at Tunhuang. This earliest dated specimen of blockprinting shows the Buddha addressing Subhuti, an aged disciple.

had done a great service to the people of China. He had gathered and translated extremely valuable information, making it available to the Chinese people for the first time.

Aftermath

Hsüan-tsang lived to be sixty-two years old. He left for India when he was twenty-seven, and returned when he was forty-two. For the last twenty years of his life, he continued to translate and write Buddhist texts for the benefit of his fellow Chinese Buddhists.

Setting a great example. Hsüan-tsang's successful travels had shown that China could benefit from contact with other peoples. As a result, China initiated trade with neighboring countries, exchanging not only goods but also ideas. The emperor T'ai Tsung allowed the citizens of China to choose their own religions. He resolved to be more receptive to Buddhism in order to keep the peace, while expanding the empire to include the largely Buddhist areas of the Tarim River basin. His tolerance toward Buddhism also made it possible to establish political relations with India, which brought new ideas in mathematics, astronomy, and medicine to China. A renewed interest in the arts such as literature and sculpture initiated a "golden age" of scholarship and art that lasted from the early 600s to about 880 A.D. Education and literacy spread, and T'ai Tsung founded a library and various colleges in the capital city. For the first time, a census was instituted to monitor the population, and government officials were recruited almost entirely by examination, rather than by appointment. Hsüan-tsang had been instrumental in opening China's borders to the new ideas that were now helping the country to flourish.

Sanskrit and Buddhism

Once he had become fluent in Sanskrit, Hsüan-tsang was able to understand the Buddhist manuscripts he wanted to translate, and he could learn about the philosophies, sciences, and arts that were also created in India. Many of the ideas that were part of Indian culture were more advanced than those in China. Hsüan-tsang brought home records of Indian science, mathematics, and literature and thus advanced Chinese learning in these areas.

Storing the records. When Hsüan-tsang returned from India, he wanted a safe place to store all of the sacred Buddhist texts and relics he had brought home. In 652 he built the Tayen Pagoda at the Ximing Monastery, where all of the items were stored, and where he translated pages and pages of Buddhist text from Sanskrit to Chinese.

Buddhism. Although Buddhism was very important to the advancement of Chinese culture, it was seen by some as being harmful to the Chinese government. Most government officials believed in Confucian philosophy. According to their beliefs, the empire was the most important thing; Buddhists, however, believed that religion was primary. Also, Buddhist monks and nuns became celibate, and they also lived at monasteries that did not pay taxes. The Chinese government needed its citizens to raise children who could become soldiers to protect the empire and they also needed tax money to support government spending. Buddhism, the Chinese rulers believed, deprived them of these things.

After T'ai Tsung, the T'ang dynasty became involved in a civil war. Although the rebellion was put down, the government was weakened and in financial trouble. Buddhists, whose temples had become wealthy, became less popular. In the 700s the emperors confiscated some of the Buddhist properties. Then, in 835, a decree was issued that limited future ordination of Buddhist monks. In 845 a Taoist emperor issued a decree that ordered temples demolished, seized Buddhist lands, and returned displaced monks and nuns to secular life. Although Buddhism continued to be an important religion for the people of China, the government continued to encourage the ideas of Confucius.

For More Information

Garraty, John A., and Peter Gray, editors. *The Columbia History of the World.* New York: Dorset, 1972.

Hookham, Hilda. *A Short History of China.* New York: St. Martin's Press, 1970.

Meyer, Milton W. *History of the Far East.* New York: Barnes and Noble, 1972.

Yap, Young, and Arthur Cotterell. *The Early Civilization of China,* New York: G.P. Putnam's Sons, 1975.

Aryabhata I

476-?

Personal Background

India in Aryabhata's time. After the death of the prominent Indian king Asoka in the early third century B.C., the unification of what is now India and Pakistan dissolved. Many factions began to struggle for power, and the empire soon broke into a number of small kingdoms. Some historians estimate that there were as many as 138 Indian kingdoms in Aryabhata I's time—each struggling to survive and to expand their territories. The people were not one common mass, but called themselves by names associated with their local government organizations.

Since that time, India has been reorganized several times and place names have changed, making the history of India an interesting puzzle. Students of Indian history have, for example, long debated such matters as where Aryabhata was born, or even where he taught and wrote his famous book, the *Aryabhatiya*. Wherever it was, the language of the scholars was Sanskrit, an ancient and complex language and script of his day. It is, however, from Aryabhata's own writing in Sanskrit that modern students have gathered the most clues about his early life.

Early life. Historians writing in the century after Aryabhata's death say that he belonged to a people who called themselves Asmaka. He was probably born and raised in the state of Asmaka Janapada in a region known as Kusumapura (or Magadha) or in

▲ A nineteenth-century depiction of an Indian scholar; much of what Aryabhata I wrote about in the sixth century seems common today.

Event: Spreading Indian mathematics and astronomy.

Role: Aryabhata developed a number system using letters and letter combinations to describe the sizes and distances of objects very accurately. He published his knowledge of arithmetic, algebra, business mathematics, and astronomy in a book of poetry called *Aryabhatiya*.

Pataliputra (the capital of the state governed by King Buddhagupta), in the northeastern corner of present-day India, west of Bangladesh and south of Nepal. Scholars agree that they know, almost to the day, the time at which Aryabhata was born. They take their clue from his own writing: "When sixty times sixty and three quarters-yugas had elapsed of the current yuga, twenty-three years had passed since my birth" (Shukla and Sarma, pp. xix-xx).

From this, historians understand that Aryabhata was twenty-three in the year 3600 of the Indian "Kali" calendar, which corresponds to the year A.D. 499 in the Western calendar. Thus Aryabhata was born in A.D. 476. Other clues tells us that his birth date was probably March 21.

Participation: Spreading Indian Mathematics and Astronomy

The Aryabhatiya. Aryabhata studied astronomy, possibly at the prestigious University of Nalanda in Pataliputra (which is probably today's city of Patna in the district of Bihar [old Magadha]). After his university years, a graduate was supposed to teach, so Aryabhata became a teacher of astronomy. Perhaps the young Aryabhata was unhappy with the materials he had for teaching. At any rate, he set out to write a book to be used by his students. Writing in the Sanskrit language, he began by defining basic arithmetic terms and facts about astronomy that he might expect his students to memorize early in their studies. His book, completed in 499, would discuss his own knowledge of mathematics, calculating time, and the shape of objects in the "celestial sphere."

By today's standards the *Aryabhatiya* would be considered a strange textbook. Although it provides instruction in arithmetic and astronomy, it was written in verse, on palm leaves. The first thirteen stanzas consist of facts that students need to know in order to understand the rest of the book. Because Aryabhata thought his students should know a shorthand way to write numerals, he invented a number system for the book based on the Sanskrit alphabet. For example, the first five consonants of the alphabet are *k, kh, g, gh,* and *n;* in Aryabhata's number system, *k* equals 1, *kh* equals 2, *g* equals 3, *gh* equals 4, *n* equals 5, and so on.

When the readers had learned all this basic information, thirty-one more stanzas of this long poem taught them about mathematics—geometry, equations, square roots, cube roots, and trigonometry.

Twenty-five stanzas taught about time. Readers learned, for example, that 1 day equals 15 manus and 1 manu equals 72 yugas. Aryabhata had calculated the length of a day to be equal to just over 23 hours, 56 minutes, and 4 seconds, although the units he used were not hours, minutes, and seconds.

After all this preparation, Aryabhata's students were ready to study the important ideas of astronomy, or what Aryabhata had learned or discovered about the movements of the sun, moon, and planets. Readers were shown how to determine when a particular planet would appear and when an eclipse was likely.

Correct judgments and errors. Aryabhata could correctly predict eclipses. He made measurements of the diameter of circles and compared them to the circumferences so accurately that his value of *pi* is still used today for everyday calculations. On the other hand, Aryabhata, like many people of his day, falsely believed that the earth, planets, sun, moon, and stars were in fixed positions in space. Though he correctly thought that the earth itself rotated, he believed that the earth's rotation made the sun, moon, and planets appear to be in different places at different times. Since the planets were fixed in space, he reasoned, he could measure them by comparing their sizes with the moon. Thus, Aryabhata concluded, if the moon is one unit across, Mars would be one-twenty-fifth of a unit, Saturn one-twentieth, Mercury one-fifteenth, Jupiter one-tenth, and Venus one-fifth.

A most exact scientist. Much of what Aryabhata wrote about seems common to students today. In his time, however, these ideas were sometimes new and sometimes refinements of

---

Mathematics in the *Aryabhatiya*

Finding the Area of a Triangle. The product of the perpendicular and half the base gives the measure of the area of a triangle.

A Problem to Solve. Find the number which yields 5 as a remainder when divided by 8, 4 as a remainder when divided by 9, and 1 as a remainder when divided by 7. (Verse 6 of the math section as translated in Shukla and Sarma, p. 38)

▲ A solar eclipse; though Aryabhata was able to determine the occurrences of eclipses, he still believed that the earth, planets, sun, moon, and stars were in fixed positions in space.

ideas that other people had developed. Aryabhata explained how to find the areas and volumes of geometric figures by thinking of triangles, rectangles, and other shapes as clusters of squares. He devised ways to solve simple algebraic and trigonometric equations and he explained how to use place value in his numerical expressions and in problem solving. Aryabhata explained how to find square roots and cube roots and to calculate interest. He also used his mathematical ideas to make accurate tables of the apparent movement of the sun.

In his time, Aryabhata was the leading mathematician and astronomer, gifted with scientific insight and foresight. A true man of science, he didn't cling to the older beliefs regarding the creation of the earth, nor did he accept forecasts of the final destruction of the world. To him, it was possible to think of things without beginning or end: he believed that the earth was everlasting.

Aftermath

The book. The *Aryabhatiya* was so popular that Aryabhata developed a following among astronomers of his time. A school of astronomy was named after him, and his book was used as a guide to astronomy for four hundred years after his death. It was published in the original language in the thirteenth century in Europe and later in Latin. In this way, the mathematical and astronomical ideas of Aryabhata influenced the sciences of Europe.

Remembering in recent years. In 1976 the first Indian spacecraft was launched on a date that fell near the fifteen hundredth anniversary of the birth of Aryabhata. The satellite, which still circles the earth beaming down information about the universe, was named "Aryabhata" in honor of the great mathematician and astronomer.

For More Information

Menon, K. N. *Aryabhata: Astronomer, Mathematician.* New Delhi, India: Ministry of Information and Broadcasting, Government of India, 1977.

Sengupta, Prabodhehandra. *Aryabhata, The Father of Indian Epicyclical Astronomy.* Calcutta, India: Calcutta University Press, 1928.

Shukla, Kilpa Shankar, and K. V. Sarma. *Aryabhatiya of Aryabhata.* New Delhi, India: Indian National Science Academy, 1976.

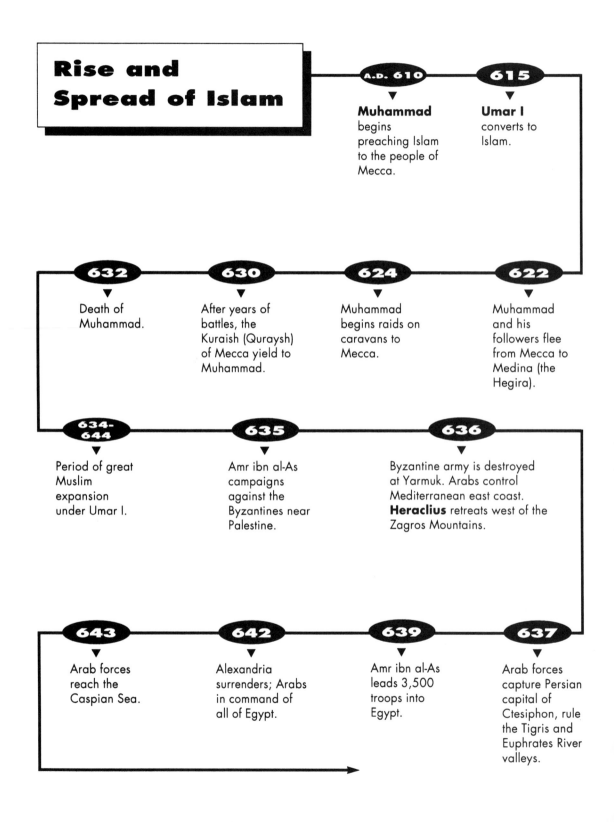

Rise and Spread of Islam

A.D. 610
Muhammad begins preaching Islam to the people of Mecca.

615
Umar I converts to Islam.

632
Death of Muhammad.

630
After years of battles, the Kuraish (Quraysh) of Mecca yield to Muhammad.

624
Muhammad begins raids on caravans to Mecca.

622
Muhammad and his followers flee from Mecca to Medina (the Hegira).

634-644
Period of great Muslim expansion under Umar I.

635
Amr ibn al-As campaigns against the Byzantines near Palestine.

636
Byzantine army is destroyed at Yarmuk. Arabs control Mediterranean east coast. **Heraclius** retreats west of the Zagros Mountains.

643
Arab forces reach the Caspian Sea.

642
Alexandria surrenders; Arabs in command of all of Egypt.

639
Amr ibn al-As leads 3,500 troops into Egypt.

637
Arab forces capture Persian capital of Ctesiphon, rule the Tigris and Euphrates River valleys.

RISE AND SPREAD OF ISLAM

In the year 610, a forty-year-old member of the trading Kuraish (also spelled Quraysh) tribe of Mecca in Arabia claimed to have received prophecies from God. He gathered together those who believed, while struggling against others in the tribe who opposed him. After a few years of toil, **Muhammad** had only gathered about forty converts. These conversions might have come to nothing except for the animosity of the powers in Mecca. By 622 the tribal leaders there had developed such hatred for Muhammad's new teachings that the prophet and his followers were forced to flee to Medina (then called Yathrib), an oasis 250 miles away.

There these followers of the new religion, Islam, found a religious tolerance that allowed them to increase in numbers. Shortly, the whole city of Medina was subject to Muhammad's rule, and he made plans to entice all the tribes in Arabia to his banner. First to be challenged was his own tribe, the Kuraish. Arousing his volunteers with strict religious rules and fiery speech, Muhammad led them to victory after victory. By 630 Muhammad's army had beaten his old foes and returned to Mecca.

Then began one of the most successful military programs of all time. Making recruits of the Arab tribesmen and exhorting them to war in the name of God, Muhammad and his successor

125

▲ A Muhammadan trading caravan and pilgrimage from Cairo to Mecca; followers of Islam must make at least one pilgrimage to Mecca during his or her lifetime.

Abu Bakr (c. 573-634) directed sweeps across Arabia and made plans to capture Palestine and Syria, where the Byzantine army of **Heraclius** strongly held the land. In short order, missionaries carried Islam by word and sword to all the Arab tribes. Following the order to always keep their backs to the friendly desert, they marched into Palestine and Syria. After a short struggle, the Byzantine emperor was forced to withdraw west of the Zagros Mountains. All of the eastern Mediterranean coast lay in the control of the people of Islam.

All the time, Muhammad and his followers, known as Muslims, were gaining a reputation for fearlessness and ruthlessness.

They extended their crusade south into Egypt. Cutting across the Nile delta, General Amr ibn al-As led his small force to the gates of the Egyptian capital at Alexandria and laid siege to the city of one million people. In seventeen months, Heraclius sent not one ship to aid the city. Finally, the governor of the city and of all of Egypt surrendered to Muslim forces.

Meanwhile, other Arab armies were attacking the Persian capital and sweeping across the mountains into central Persia. Under the direction of **Umar I,** the second caliph, the teachings of Muhammad were spread by the Koran and by war throughout Syria, Persia, and northern Africa. In less than one hundred years, the Muslims would control all of the Middle East and would begin to influence India.

Amr ibn al-As had captured Egypt and headed to Tripoli in Libya. He might have gone on to capture all of northern Africa but was recalled to Medina. The advance in Africa continued under other leaders, and by the year 700, Muslims had taken charge of all north Africa and had begun to move into Europe through Spain.

The marvelous advance would only come to a halt in France through the resistance of an equally ferocious leader, Charlemagne.

The Power of the Word

Muhammad used promise and fear to encourage the Arab fighters for Islam. The promise was of a rosy life after this earthly one for any fighter for Islam. The fear is expressed in the Islamic holy book, the Koran: "Whoever of you apostasies from his religion will die a heathen.... Their actions will be defeated in this world and the next. These are the people who will remain eternally in hell fire." (Koran 2:217)

Muhammad

c. 570-632

Personal Background

Mecca. At the end of the sixth century A.D., the Arabian peninsula was inhabited mostly by Bedouins, nomadic people who traveled from one watering place to another, herding their animals and adding to their income by raiding one another. In a few places, settled towns had taken shape at sites of trade, since the Arabs had already established a brisk trade with Persia and other cities of the north.

One of these trading centers was Mecca, in present-day western Saudi Arabia and situated about fifty miles inland from the Red Sea. Founded along caravan trails in a spot with no natural wealth, Mecca thrived as a place of commerce. The normally warring Bedouin tribes gathered here in peace to trade with local merchants, who in turn organized great camel caravans bound for trade in the north.

Not only was Mecca an important commercial center, it was renowned for its religious significance. One attraction was a square arrangement of rocks called the Kaaba—a place where the various tribes placed idols of their gods—which contained a black rock said to have been brought there by the Hebrew patriarch Abraham when he first built the holy place in the early second millennium B.C. During holy days, fighting among tribes was banned in Mecca, and visitors from all around Arabia came to the

▲ Muhammad

Event: The beginning of Islam.

Role: Claiming to have been called by God to become his messenger and final prophet, Muhammad united the nomadic tribes of the Arabian peninsula. He established a simple set of rules for his followers that grew to encompass every aspect of life. After his death, these laws, gathered into an organized holy book, the Koran, spread throughout the Middle East, Africa, and eventually the world and became the basic tenets of a new religion, Islam.

▲ The Kaaba at Mecca, which contains a black rock said to have been brought there by the Hebrew patriarch Abraham.

Kaaba to worship their gods. So holy was this place that those fortunate enough to live in Mecca were given to walking around the Kaaba seven times each day.

The family of Muhammad. Mecca had another attraction, a well whose water was said to have great religious and healing properties. As with most of the businesses of Mecca, this well was controlled by a single tribe, the Kuraish ("sharks"). The keeper of the well was a Kuraish chieftain named Ahd-al Muttalib. His son Abdallah was, in turn, a fairly successful camel driver who hired out to the various caravans traveling through Mecca. Young and handsome, Abdallah attracted the young women of Mecca but was himself attracted to Amina. The two lived together as husband and wife.

About the year 570, Abdallah set out on one of the caravans to an oasis called Yathrib, 210 miles north of Mecca. He never returned. Abdallah became ill and died in Yathrib, never having seen the son that Amina soon bore him. The boy's grandfather gave him the name Muhammad, a term meaning "praiseworthy." Some thought it was an unusually impressive name for a boy born in such lowly circumstances.

Early life. Muhammad did not have a smooth start in life. His mother was unable to care for him, so as a baby he was given to Halima, a nursemaid of another tribe. Halima took Muhammad to live outside Mecca with her nomadic tribe but returned him to his mother after a few years—some say because the child was given to epileptic fits.

The return to his real mother, whom he had never really known, was frightening to the boy. At age five he ran away, only to be found and returned by a friendly uncle. A year later, mother and son headed off to Yathrib, perhaps to visit the grave of his father. But Amina suffered the same fate as the boy's father—at Yathrib she became deathly ill. Hurriedly, mother, son, and a female slave rushed back toward their home in Mecca, but Amina died on the way. The slave woman brought the six-year-old Muhammad back to his grandfather.

It was customary for tribes to take care of their own and for the family clans into which the tribes were divided to take responsibilities for their families. Muhammad, therefore, came into the care of a kindly uncle, Abu Talib.

Education. Owing to the instability of his early life, Muhammad probably had little education. He later claimed that he could not read until he was commanded to do so by a representative of God who spoke to him in a vision. However, he did learn careful attention to detail, and this made him valuable in planning caravans. And he was so faithful in carrying out his responsibilities that, even as a young man, he was known by his nickname, al-Amin—"The Trusty."

Muhammad may have become a camel driver like his father and participated in trading trips as far away as Yemen in the south and Syria in the north. But living in Mecca, where many peoples crossed paths, and traveling the trade routes, Muhammad had many opportunities to observe Arab tribes as well as the Christians and Jews who often passed through in the caravans.

Far to the north in the Byzantine Empire, religion had become the hottest topic of conversation. People everywhere were debating the real nature of God and of Jesus Christ. Muhammad probably spent many evenings around a campfire listening to stories of two other great religions, Christianity and Judaism.

Marriage. Muhammad grew to be a rather handsome young man. He was of average height and lighter-skinned than many of his friends. His brilliant black hair was always carefully tended. His teeth were also well cared for and seemed to be filed into points, as was the practice of some men of his day. He was quiet and shy; according to his own story, Muhammad never touched a woman until he had the good fortune to meet Kahdija.

Muhammad was twenty-five when Kahdija, a wealthy banker, noticed his good looks and his kind and gentle manners. She is said to have been forty years old and twice widowed. The story is that Kahdija proposed marriage and Muhammad accepted. The two lived together happily until Kahdija's death twenty-five years later.

Participation: The Beginning of Islam

Visions. When Muhammad was a boy he had had a religious vision. He experienced no others until he was an adult, when he began to have them from time to time. Some of these revelations took place in a cave under Mt. Hira, north of Mecca, where he would often retreat to think. During his most important vision, the voice of the angel Gabriel commanded him to read a message. Though Muhammad protested that he could not read, he was suddenly able to. The message called Muhammad to be the messenger of God and to teach that there was but one God and no other. He immediately set out to spread God's word as it was revealed to him. He was forty years old.

Family support. A few relatives immediately supported Muhammad in his work, but after four years of telling about his encounter with Gabriel, he had made only about forty converts. Muhammad did, however, make a larger number of enemies, for the new teachings were very strange to the Arab tribes. They were asked to abandon the more than one hundred gods whose icons rested in the Kaaba. Even more difficult, Muhammad also wanted them to recognize him as God's messenger—the last ever in the long line of prophets that began with the Hebrew patriarch Abraham and included the prophets of the ancient Jews as well as Jesus Christ of the Christians.

Muhammad and Abraham

Muhammad traced his ancestry and his religion to the ancient leader Abraham—the same Abraham the Jews claimed as their founder. Certainly, Muhammad instructed his warriors as the biblical characters did the earlier warriors: "Thou shalt consume all the people which the Lord thy God shall deliver thee; thine eye shall have no pity upon them." (Deuteronomy 6:16)

Heaven and hell. Nine years passed after the visit of Gabriel before Muhammad's next major dream. He dreamed that he traveled on a white animal to a place where he met with all the prophets of old. He was surprised that he and Abraham looked strikingly similar. After meeting with the prophets, he left to find "Jacob's ladder." In his dream, Muhammad climbed the ladder through seven heavens and saw the grandeur of paradise. He was then shown a view of hell, where poisonous gases rose high into the air. One translation gives Muhammad's personal account of the sight: "I saw men with lips like camels. In their hands were lumps of fiery stone which they thrust into their mouths, and they would come out of their posteriors. I was told that these were once men who had sinfully devoured the wealth of orphans" (Kelen, p. 78).

The dream, which later became known as the "Night Journey" story and inspired another tenet of Islam, seemed so unbelievable to the people of Mecca that some of Muhammad's followers left him and the town ridiculed his ideas more than ever. One of his relatives heard the story and thought it strange. But such was Muhammad's reputation for honesty and purity of heart that when the same relative learned the source of the "Night Journey" story, he allowed that if Muhammad said it, it was certainly true.

Hegira. By 622 conditions in Mecca had become unbearable for Muhammad's followers. He was disturbed that he had not won more followers, and his opponents were becoming increasingly alarmed that his words would disrupt their own ways of life. As opposition grew into threats on his life, help came from Yathrib.

Yathrib had become a thriving agricultural town and had attracted several Bedouin, Christian, and Jewish tribes to settle there. But there was constant squabbling and fighting among the tribes. Some of the leaders thought that a permanent peacemaker would help, so they invited Muhammad to move there. After two years' thought and with the agreement that the major tribes of Yathrib would support him, Muhammad directed his few followers to move to Yathrib. From that time on, the town was known as Medina (an abbreviation of Medinat un-Nabi, "City of the Prophet"). The movement from Mecca to Medina is known as the Hegira (also spelled hijra) and marks the beginning of the Muslim calendar.

> **The Call to Prayer**
>
> Five times daily, callers climb the open columns (minarets) of the Muslim mosques and call believers to prayer: "God is most great. I testify that there is no God but Allah. I testify that Muhammad is God's Apostle. Come to prayer, come to security. God is most great." (Wallbank, Taylor, and Bailkey p. 251)

Life in Medina. With little agricultural land, the city of Mecca had been filled with business people, bankers, and traders. Medina, on the other hand, had several springs, each controlled by one or more tribes who grew dates and other foods. It was a strange world for the people of Islam. Not understanding agriculture, they were forced to try their hand at the business of the city. In this they competed directly with the three Jewish tribes who were both farmers and businessmen. Almost immediately, friction developed between Muslims and Jews. The Jews never claimed to support the Muslim immigrants and resented their intrusion into Medina's affairs. The quarreling between the two groups would eventually lead to the eviction of Jews from Medina.

The five pillars of faith. Whenever a problem occurred, Muhammad retreated into meditation to receive a solution from

God. One thing that concerned him was increasing the number of his followers. Missionaries needed to be trained to convert the Bedouin tribes, who could strengthen the Muslims' protection against their enemies. In order to make it easier to train missionaries, Muhammad wrote down the five major tenets of Islam in a sort of lyrical language. As with most of his teachings, he had them written on whatever bits of scrap or leaf could be found:

- Confess the faith: There is no God but God, and Muhammad is His Prophet.

- Pray daily. (This changed to praying five times daily.)

- Give alms to the needy. (God told Muhammad: "They will ask you what they shall bestow in alms; tell them, what they can spare.")

- Fast from sunup to sundown for the holy month, Ramadan.

- Make at least one pilgrimage to Mecca in your lifetime.

Some of these five teachings seem to have been made in an attempt to reconcile the early Islam to the activities of their Jewish neighbors. They became the five pillars of Islamic faith.

Muhammad on Marriage

Muhammad encouraged Muslim men to take only a number of wives they could support equally and well. But this advice sometimes conflicted with the wildness of the desert, in which everyone needed protection. Marrying was one way to ensure cooperation and defense. Muhammad himself married other women after Kahdija. All, like Kahdija, were widows, except for a nine-year-old girl. It seems that he was moved to marry these women as much for their protection as for their company. The names of Muhammad's wives were: Kahdija, Sawda, Ayeda, Hafsa, Zayueb, Uma Salama, Zaynab bint Jarsh, Jawayriya, Umm Habiba, Safiyya, and Maymuna.

Summa. As time passed and new problems arose, other rules more directed toward correct everyday living were also revealed to the Prophet: It is difficult to treat more than one wife impartially; If you leave home to earn your living, leave home kindly; Waste not, for the wasteful are Satan's own brothers; If anyone has trouble repaying a loan, grant a delay until it be easier for him (Kelen, pp. 239-40). There were also more direct rules, such as do not eat pork; do not drink alcohol; wash before prayers. These rules and others that offered a guide to everyday conduct grew into a body of laws called the *Summa*.

These and other rules of conduct, the five pillars, and illustrative stories of Islamic ancestors from Abraham through Ishmael and the prophets to Muhammad were collected, after the Prophet's death, and compiled into the Summa and the Islamic holy book, the Koran (or Qur'an). The early Muslims recognized the value of an adversary in rallying supporters. So the Koran began with unfavorable comments about Jews and Christians, whom Muhammad felt had strayed from God's path.

Turning to violence. As the quarreling between groups in Medina intensified, the community grew divided. There were the Jews; the Arab tribes who had become "Helpers" of the Muslims; and a small group of true followers, the "Emigrants," who had followed Muhammad from Mecca. Unaccustomed to farming and new to the Medina business people, the Emigrants found earning a living difficult and received little help from the other two groups. Within a year or two after the Hegira, God revealed to Muhammad an option—the Emigrants were allowed to raid and fight for what they needed.

Muhammad had always been known for his nonviolent nature. As a young man, he had preferred the dangerous task of collecting enemy arrows and resupplying the fighters for Mecca to actually using the weapons himself. He found this new revelation difficult. In fact, personally leading his fighters on two of their first four raids, he turned back upon seeing the plight of the long-distance travelers and their caravans. Finally the Muslims did attack a large caravan traveling to Mecca. The caravan escaped, but word had reached Mecca of the raiding plan, and an army was sent to do battle. About 600 Meccans and their allies confronted the 86 Emigrants and their 238 Helpers in the battle of Badr on March 15, 624, in the midst of the holy month. (Their very practical God told them that fighting during the holy month was a serious matter, but starving was more serious.) The Muslims' victory over the superior force won Islam great prestige and

▶
A sixteenth-century Iranian miniature depicting Muhammad ascending to Paradise.

many converts. Muhammad's power and the Islamic religion began to spread throughout Arabia.

Mecca and the Bedouin tribes. In 625 an army of three thousand Meccans confronted about seven hundred followers of Muhammad at Uhud. This battle was not conclusive, and ill will remained. Nevertheless, soon after the battle, Muhammad decided to brave the opposition and travel to Mecca to do the ritual walk around the Kaaba. It was 629 before he was allowed to do that. By 630, however, Muhammad and his growing band of followers marched against Mecca, which fell without a fight. One of the conditions of the agreement that would end hostilities would have lasting effects: the Meccan tribes allowed Muhammad to have free access to the nomadic Bedouin tribes. Muhammad had already begun making use of this freedom: Bedouin tribes, weary of fighting one another and looking for some common ground, were visited by Muslim missionaries and accepted Islam as their moral code. The Muslim Bedouins would become the warriors in the *jihad* (holy war) that would soon carry Islam to Syria, the Byzantine Empire, Africa, and eventually Europe.

Aftermath

Death. On June 8, 632, Muhammad became ill and was carried to the hut of his third wife, Aishah (he took eight after the death of his first wife). He died in her arms. True believers found his death difficult to accept. One of the most faithful leaders, **Umar I** (see entry), was speaking to a congregation when he heard the news. "There may be some hypocrites here who will try to tell you that the Prophet is dead; but, by God, he is not dead," he said (Kelen, p. 257).

Islam. Umar had spoken from emotion. A wiser man, also a leader of the Muslims, then spoke, "O men, if anyone has come here to worship Muhammad, Muhammad is dead. If anyone is here to worship God, God is alive and immortal" (Kelen, p. 257). This man, Abu Bakr, was elected leader of the Muslims. He made no claim, however, of being a prophet. His title as head of the religion was "caliph," or "successor."

Abu Bakr spent the rest of his life putting down rebellions among the Muslims. After his death, the Muslims divided. Those who felt that Ali, Muhammad's adopted son, should be the leader broke away from the major body of Muslims and became today's Shiite sect. The destroyers of Abu Bakr, the Umayyads, established a dynasty, set up a new caliph, and became the Sunni sect. Today, the Shiites hold power in lower Iraq and Iran while the Sunni sect controls most of the Muslim world.

For More Information

Arberry, A. J. *The Holy Koran.* London: Aris and Phillips, 1953.

Glubb, John Bagot. *The Life and Times of Muhammad.* New York: Stein and Day, 1970.

Hitti, Philip K. *History of the Arabs.* New York: St. Martin's, 1964.

Kelen, Betty. *Muhammad: The Messenger of God.* Nashville, Tennessee: Thomas Nelson, 1975.

The Student Bible. New International Version. Grand Rapids, Michigan: Zondervan, 1992.

Wallbank, T. Walter, Alastair M. Taylor, and Nels M. Bailkey. *Civilization: Past and Present.* 5th edition. Vol. 1. Chicago, Illinois: Scott, Foresman, 1965.

Umar I

c. 586-644

Personal Background

The family of Umar. Umar ibn al-Khattab (Umar son of Khattab) was born in Mecca in present-day western Saudi Arabia, about fifty miles inland from the Red Sea. Born in 586, sixteen years after the prophet **Muhammad** (see entry) was born, Umar was, in fact, from the same tribe as Muhammad, the Kuraish. Mecca was dominated by the Kuraish tribe, which consisted of thirty-six clans. The Kuraish owned most of the stone buildings in Mecca and also controlled the religious shrine, the Kaaba, in the center of town. Within the tribe of Kuraish, Umar was from the clan of Adi ibn Kaab (or Adi son of Kaab), which was a powerful and important one in Mecca and served a special function as envoys and arbitrators in cases of dispute.

Childhood. Being from Mecca's merchant upper class, Umar was considered well educated, meaning that he knew how to read and write. Because there were many clans who were Christian and Jewish, he undoubtedly was familiar with their religious traditions and probably incorporated them into his family's religion, which included veneration of several gods. He was, like most Arabs at the time, intensely fond of and loyal to his family and became an expert in genealogy. In his early adolescence, he helped his family on the battlefield, probably picking up arrows for the family warriors to reuse.

▲ A modern mosque in Cairo; Umar I and the other exiled Muslims built the first mosque in Medina.

Event: The rise and spread of Islam.

Role: Umar I was the second caliph (successor) to lead Islam after the prophet Muhammad. For ten years, from 634 to 644, Umar directed the Muslim crusade against the Byzantine Empire of Heraclius to the border of India and across Egypt to all of northern Africa.

Umar grew up in an aristocratic household and learned the business of a merchant like the rest of his family. By his mid-twenties, he had struck out on his own, started a new family, and begun organizing camel caravans.

Personality. Umar was quick to anger and given to violent acts. A tall and powerfully built man from the Meccan ruling class, he became a respected and feared warrior in the local tribal warfare and defenses against raids of Meccan caravans. He was feared on the battlefield but also feared on the streets of Mecca. It was said that his walking staff was more terrible than most men's swords.

When Muhammad began preaching Islam to the people of Mecca around 610, Umar joined in the growing opposition to the new religion, but those around him, including his cousin and even his sister, attended secret meetings to study the Muslim holy book, the Koran (Qur'an). As Islam became more popular among the young, poor, and outcast in Mecca, the atmosphere in the city became tense.

Conversion. One day around the year 615, Umar discovered that secret meetings to study the Koran were taking place at the house of a young convert named al-Arqam. In his early thirties and as quick-tempered as ever, Umar grabbed his sword and stormed out of the house, intending to break up the meeting and kill Muhammad. On the way, an old man told him that his brother-in-law Saeed and sister Fatima had become Muslims. Umar quickly turned around and, still in a rage, ran to his sister's house, where people were, at the time, studying the Prophet's words. Umar stormed in, began hitting Saeed and Fatima and screaming.

Fatima, with blood running down her face cried, "Yes, we are Muslims, we believe in God and His Messenger and you can do what you like." Umar saw the violence and anger he had created and his rage suddenly vanished. He said, "Give me what you

►

A page from the Koran; Umar read some of the Muslim holy book and, dumbstruck, proclaimed, "What splendid words are these."

were reading, so that I can see what Muhammad says." Umar read some of the Koran and, dumbstruck, proclaimed, "What splendid words are these."

He hurried back to the house of al-Arqam. Muhammad, however, opened the door and challenged, "When will you cease your persecutions, O Umar?" Umar, having found the one thing that could tame his rages and pride, replied meekly, "O Apostle of God, I have come to you to believe in God and his Apostle." Umar converted and quickly became one of Muhammad's closest lieutenants (Glubb, p. 123).

Participation: The Rise and Spread of Islam

Exile from Mecca. Despite the continuing persecution in Mecca, Islam began to spread slowly to the surrounding tribes and communities. In 622 the situation in Mecca became too dangerous, and the Muslims decided to flee to Yathrib on the invitation of some of Yathrib's leaders. Umar was among the first to go, being selected to help settle the community before Muhammad arrived. Flaunting danger and defying the Meccan rulers, Umar led about twenty other followers out of Mecca in broad daylight. At the age of thirty-nine, he sacrificed his wealth, career, and status for his faith in Islam.

The new Islamic community soon gathered members from Yathrib (called Medina after the arrival of the Muslims) and other towns and tribes. Muhammad and his two closest lieutenants, Umar and Abu Bakr (c. 573-634), welded the exiled Meccans and the Medinian tribes into a community based on the will of God as revealed through Muhammad and on the common law of the tribesmen.

Aid from Medina to the Muslims was not as plentiful as the leaders had hoped. After only seven months of exile, the Meccans were nearly out of food. In desperation, they decided to raid caravans of the Kuraish, who had primarily been responsible for driving them out of Mecca in the first place. Umar, naturally, became one of the leaders of these first raids, which quickly escalated into virtual war with Mecca, the Kuraish stronghold. At the same time,

Muhammad's power and the Islamic religion began to spread throughout Arabia. Umar sent messengers to the tribes in efforts to convert more of them and convince the tribes not to fight among themselves. Umar remained one of Muhammad's top generals through the battles with the Kuraish of Mecca. Finally victorious, the Muslims triumphantly marched into Mecca in 630.

Islam's success in Arabia. The taking of Mecca solidified Muhammad and his followers as the main power in Arabia. Where it once had been dangerous to follow Islam and its one God, Allah, it was now dangerous to be a polytheist (worshipper of the many gods in the old tribal religions). Muhammad and his generals declared war on all polytheistic tribes in Arabia. The idea attracted many soldiers, who were always searching for a chance to loot. In 631 representatives from all over Arabia came to Muhammad to declare their faith and loyalty to the new religion and to prove their loyalty by paying their *zakat*, or income tax. Islam quickly turned into an empire embracing cities and towns populated by not only converts but also Christians and Jews. These non-Muslims were obliged to pay a poll-tax, or *jizyah*, in addition to the *zakat*.

Not all followers were convinced believers. Bedouin tribes, who saw Muhammad as just another new prince, "converted" to Islam for their own material gain after the visit of one of Muhammad's generals. These tribes needed to be held under close watch, so Muhammad needed powerful allies whom he could trust. He drew Umar closer to him than ever before, even taking Umar's daughter Hafsa as one of his wives.

Death of Muhammad. Muhammad had nearly unified Arabia under his control when he became deathly ill in 632. Fearing rivalry between his two closest companions, Abu Bakr and Umar, he ordered Abu Bakr to act as *imam* and lead the community of Medina in prayer. Muhammad lingered another ten days before he died.

The First Years in Medina

The early exile period was also extremely important in the development of Islam as a religion. It was at this time that the first mosque was built, the five daily prayers were developed, and other rituals were standardized. Muhammad had a vision in which he saw a man reciting the Adham, the Muslim call to prayers. Umar suggested that a man should be appointed to do it, and that form of call was ultimately adopted.

When news of Muhammad's death broke, a crowd gathered outside the mosque, a few already beginning to waiver in their belief. Umar, furious that the community would say anything against the Prophet, declared that the Prophet was not dead but had just left temporarily, as the Hebrew prophet Moses had done centuries earlier. Abu Bakr, however, then came to the crowd and told them that Muhammad was indeed dead, but that the religion lived.

Abu Bakr and Umar went back inside the mosque to continue praying, while the crowd then went to the council hall to discuss the election of a new ruler. When Umar and Abu Bakr heard about this, they rushed over to the meeting. Umar stood up and declared that the rule properly belonged to Abu Bakr, that Muhammad choose Abu Bakr as *imam* during his sickness. By evening Abu Bakr was elected the new leader by acclamation and given the title of "caliph," or "successor." Umar was his right-hand man, organizing his army.

Khalid quells rebellions. Muhammad's death sent shock waves throughout Arabia, and the unity that he created quickly fell apart. Various tribes stopped paying taxes, and the country was in revolt. Most of Abu Bakr's short reign was spent trying to reunify Arabia. He immediately sent out an army under the young general Khalid ibn al-Walid, a shrewd, ruthless, vain, and brilliant leader who once said that "the taste of blood is pleasant on my mouth" (Payne, p. 90). Umar hated him. By now Umar's years of devotion and leadership in Islam had made him strict and disciplined. Khalid was extravagant; Umar was simple. It had become a common sight in Medina to see Umar take his meal of barley and water on the steps of the mosque. This simple and strict way of living earned him respect and the loyalty of his troops.

Khalid, however, was brilliantly successful in putting down the rebellions. After Arabia was reunified, Umar's armies were still restless. They could no longer fight against themselves, since all Arabian tribes were now Muslim and it was a sin to kill another of the faith. Muhammad, however, had left a very specific order to his successors: "After us, you will conquer Syria and Persia" (Davis, p. 126). The Byzantine and Persian empires were extremely weak from years of fighting each other. The Byzantine emperor **Heraclius** (see entry) had reconquered Syria and Egypt from the Persians only a few years earlier, and the Persians were in a state of anarchy with no permanent ruler. In 633 Abu Bakr declared a Holy War, or *jihad,* against Syria and sent the bulk of the army into Syria and a smaller column, led by Khalid, into Persia.

Death of Abu Bakr. Khalid headed north and raided the southern bank of the Euphrates, taking a number of small towns including Hirah, and then turned south to support the army in Syria. After a grueling eighteen-day march from the Euphrates to Palestine, the combined Muslim army met Theodore, Heraclius's brother, and his army at Ajnadayn in present-day Palestine. The fierce battle broke the Byzantines, and the whole of Palestine was taken under Islamic rule. Abu Bakr, however, did not live long enough to savor the victory. After fifteen days of fever, he died on August 23, 634. On his deathbed, Abu Bakr requested that Umar become the second caliph.

Conquest of Syria. Islam had now had a number of military successes, but its struggles were far from over. Shortly after the death of Abu Bakr, Khalid took Damascus, the key city in Syria. Heraclius, however, was determined to finish the Arabs once and for all and amassed a huge army at Antioch. After two years of small raids back and forth, the main armies finally met each other on August 20, 636, in the hottest month in one of the hottest places on earth: the mouth of the Jordan valley at Yarmuk. Shortly after the battle began, a thick dust storm darkened the sky. The heat and dust, along with the piercing arrows of the Arabs, panicked the Byzantine troops. Theodore was killed and the army scattered. Islam was once again victorious, and Heraclius abandoned Syria to the Muslims.

The Early Caliphs and Years of Their Caliphates

Abu Bakr,
father-in-law and best friend of Muhammad
632-634

Umar ibn al-Khattab (Umar I),
an early opponent of Muhammad
634-644

Uthman ibn Affan,
from a wealthy branch of the Kuraish tribe of Mecca
644-654

Ali ibn Abi Talib,
adopted son of Muhammad
656-661

After Yathrib, it was simply a matter of time before the other major cities and the Mediterranean coast were taken. Jerusalem and the port of Caesarea (Qisarya) defended themselves in vain. When Jerusalem, the ancient holy city, fell in 638, Sophronius, the Patriarch of Jerusalem, and the other town elders insisted that Caliph Umar himself come to sign the treaty. Umar entered Jerusalem on a camel with only a few attendants and in his usual old, dust-stained, patched clothes, giving the impression of simplicity itself. He was met by Khalid, Amr ibn al-As, and his other generals decked out in silken robes from the booty they had taken. When Khalid remarked that it was unworthy for the caliph to be dressed in such somber clothes, Umar flew into a rage: "How dare ye show yourselves to me while thus arrayed?" (Davis, p. 132).

The Wealth of Umar and of Islam

Although Umar preferred a simple life, and for much of his life even went without shoes, he was very protective of the wealth gained for Islam in combat. Arab soldiers were paid with the booty they captured, except that one-fifth of all the wealth gained went directly to the leaders of Islam. This wealth Umar guarded closely, even sending special investigators to watch such field generals as Amr ibn al-As when Umar suspected that not enough money was coming from Egypt.

Conquest of Mesopotamia and Persia. The action in Persia took a different turn. Shortly after Umar had been appointed caliph, the Arab army was severely defeated at the Battle of the Bridge, where they proved to be no match for the Persian elephants. The northern army spent the next two years under the Bedouin general Muthanna harassing the Persians from their base at Hira (near present-day An Najaf, Iraq). Umar then raised another army under Sa'd ibn-abi-Waqqas, one of the oldest of Muhammad's companions. In 637 Sa'd, ready for battle, camped in the nearby village of Qadisiyah. As was his custom, Umar first sent emissaries with the word of Islam to the five-year-old Persian emperor Yazdegerd III and his advisors at the capital of Ctesiphon and offered peace if he would accept Islam and be willing to pay tribute to Medina. Amazed at Umar's gall, they sent the messengers back with sackfuls of dirt instead of tribute.

The showdown in Persia finally came to an end that summer. Rustam, the Persian field marshal, grew impatient and ordered his 120,000-strong army to move on Qadisiyah. Sa'd was ill and directed his defending army of 30,000 from his bed. The fierce battle lasted three days, most of it fought during a blinding sandstorm. The first two days looked bleak for the Arabs. On the third day, however, the storm was especially heavy and a small band succeeded in making it to Rustam's command post and killing him. Once word of Rustam's death reached the troops, they dissolved in panic. Mesopotamia and Persia lay open to the Arabs. For the next ten years, Muslim influence spread out across central Asia. When the immense Persian treasures reached Medina, tears of apprehension filled Umar's eyes: "I fear this wealth and comfort may ultimately cause the ruin of my people" (Ali, p. 125).

Demotion of Khalid. Umar believed the spoils and success of war would endanger Islam and that the extravagance would destroy the law of the Koran. For Umar, all power came from the Commonwealth of Islam and the Koran. Now that taxes and booty were plentiful, he worried about his leadership. "By God!" exclaimed Umar, "I know not whether I am caliph or king and it frightens me" (Ali, p. 194). To Umar, the dangers of the corruption of power was embodied in Khalid. Shortly before leaving for Jerusalem, he demoted the general, while at the same time allowing the rival general, Amr ibn al-As, to continue on into Egypt. Then, in 638, Khalid gave a thousand dinars, a very large sum, to a poet for singing of his prowess on the battlefield. Upon hearing of this, Umar became enraged and ordered Khalid back to Medina. Khalid refused to return. Umar ordered that Khalid's hands be tied with his own turban, a symbol of guilt, and brought back. Back in Medina, Khalid insisted that the money was his own. Umar forgave him but barred him from ever returning to the battlefield, explaining that he was afraid lest people should attribute the conquests of Islam to Khalid's skill and prowess when the victories were all from God. Khalid died a beggar, alone and forgotten, in 641.

Invasion of Egypt. When Amr asked permission from Umar to invade Egypt, Umar answered as he usually did to his generals: he said nothing. If the venture were successful, the general would be rewarded, if unsuccessful, punished. In December 639, Amr left Jerusalem with fewer than five thousand troops. Just as he was nearing the border of Palestine and Egypt, a message from Umar arrived. Amr decided to cross the gully before opening the letter which read: "If my letter ordering thee to turn back from Egypt overtakes thee before thou hast entered any part of the country, then turn back; but if thou hast invaded the land before receiving my letter, then proceed, and may God hold thee!" (Payne, p. 100). Having already crossed into Egypt, Amr swept into the country, capturing Pelusium and Heliopolis in 640 and 641 respectively. Alexandria, one of the prizes of the ancient world, fell in 642.

When Umar heard the news, he gave the messenger a meal of bread and dates and held a small service in the mosque in celebration. Egypt was one of the breadbaskets of the ancient world. Umar ordered a canal dug connecting the Nile with the Red Sea, which would allow easy transportation of corn to the Arabian port of Yanbu. The canal remained in use for eighty years until it became so filled with sand as to become unnavigable.

Aftermath

Organizing the empire. Within ten years, the Islamic empire had expanded from a few tribes in Arabia to a wide empire encompassing Egypt, Persia, Syria, Palestine, and the whole of the Arabian peninsula. Umar not only had to raise and organize the conquering armies and deal with the intrigues of the generals and governors, he also had to create a new bureaucracy to rule his new possessions. Although ruthless on the battlefield and zealous in his faith, Umar was not tyrannical in his rule of conquered peoples. Neither he nor the Arabs had experience in conquering and administering the new territories, and he had no desire to extract harsh terms or vast wealth. He therefore improvised, relying upon and expanding the existing bureaucracy. The Arabs, it seems, were also much more gentle toward their new subjects than either the Romans or the Persians had been. Although they offered people the opportunity to convert to Islam if they wished, the thought of forcing Islam upon everyone had not yet dawned on the Muslim mind. Umar was primarily concerned that nonbelievers pay the *jizyah,* or poll-tax, as a show of their obedience to Muslim rule.

As tax moneys poured into Medina, Umar began building the administration of the Islamic empire. The caliph sent out scores of teachers of the Koran to all the provinces. These also served as administrative liaisons to Medina. He built jails, organized a police force, appointed governors based upon merit alone, and established a census for tax purposes. Umar also introduced a new code of laws based upon the Koran and ruled with strict interpretation and severe sentences. When his son was found drunk one night, Umar had him flogged to death in accordance with his interpretation of the law.

Umar's death. One day, as Umar was entering the mosque in Medina, he was stabbed by a Persian slave, a Christian named Abu Lu'lu'ah Firoz. The day before, Umar had ruled against him in a case against his master. The wound was deep and cut Umar's bowels. The slave then turned the dagger on himself. After learning who stabbed him, Umar thanked God that he had not been killed by a fellow Muslim. He asked Aishah, Muhammad's favorite wife, that he be buried next to the Prophet as Abu Bakr had been. Aishah immediately agreed. He lingered four more days and died on November 23, 644.

For More Information

Ali, Maulana Muhammad. *Early Caliphate.* Lahore, Pakistan: Ahmadiyya Anjuman-i-Isha'at-i-Islam, 1947.

Davis, William Stearns. *A Short History of the Near East.* New York: MacMillan, 1923.

Glubb, John Bagot. *The Life and Times of Muhammad.* New York: Stein and Day, 1970.

Payne, Robert. *The Holy Sword.* New York: Harper and Brothers, 1959.

Heraclius

c. 575-641

Personal Background

Heraclius was born in Carthage, the ancient city in North Africa that had been Rome's first major enemy eight centuries earlier. Those ancient wars had ended in Carthage's defeat. Since then, the city had been part of the eastern Roman empire, later called the Byzantine Empire. (In 330 the emperor Constantine the Great chose the city of Byzantium to be the capital of the eastern Roman empire. He renamed it Constantinople.) As Heraclius grew up in Carthage, his father, also called Heraclius, led the fight against another old enemy, Persia, far to the east. The senior Heraclius proved to be the empire's most reliable general. As a reward for his service, the emperor Maurice (c. 539-602) put him in charge of Carthage and the surrounding area when peace was declared in 591. His younger brother Gregorius was second in command.

Persia attacks again. Maurice, however, was overthrown in 602. For eight years, Phocas, the man who had overthrown him, ruled the empire. During his harsh reign, the unpopular Phocas spent much of his time executing those he suspected of trying to overthrow him. When the Persians attacked again, Phocas's best general refused to fight for him. As a result, the Persians conquered much of the empire's territory and advanced toward the capital itself, the great city of Constantinople. By 608 Persian campfires could be seen from the city walls.

▲ **Heraclius**

Event: War between the Byzantine and Persian empires opens the way for Islamic conquests.

Role: Heraclius, who ruled the eastern Roman or Byzantine Empire for more than thirty years, defeated its old enemy, Persia, in 628. The long war exhausted both empires, and when the Arabs burst on the scene in the 630s, neither could offer much resistance. Rallying around the banner of their powerful young religion, Islam, the Arabs began their conquests of Byzantine and Persian lands.

A fleet sails from Carthage. After eight years of bad rule, the only part of the empire still prosperous was the area around Carthage, governed by the senior Heraclius. When he heard that the capital was in danger of being overrun by the Persian forces, he outfitted a fleet of warships and a large army. The army he put in the charge of his nephew, Gregorius's son. It set out by land on the long march eastward. The fleet he put under the command of his son Heraclius, with orders to sail for Constantinople.

Taking power. Heraclius stopped in many of the empire's major cities on his sea journey eastward. At each, he was welcomed as a hero, and his force was added to by young men eager to join it. Soon he was secretly contacted by leaders in Constantinople, who promised him that the whole population would support him if he tried to overthrow Phocas. By the time Heraclius sailed into port at Constantinople, Phocas had already been captured by Heraclius's supporters. Phocas was brought before Heraclius in chains. "And it is thus that you have governed your empire?" Heraclius demanded. "Are you sure you will be able to do any better?" Phocas responded (Jenkins, p. 20). Heraclius ordered him executed. Later that afternoon, Heraclius married his long-time fiancee, Eudocia. Right after the wedding, he was crowned emperor.

Participation:
Opens the Way for Islamic Conquests

Rebuilding an empire. Heraclius faced huge problems at the beginning of his reign, both inside and outside the empire. The imperial government had no money, its officials were corrupt and lazy, and the army lacked any kind of fighting spirit or discipline. Furthermore, the empire was threatened by dangerous neighbors not only to the east, where Persia lay, but to the west as well, where the Avars and other barbarian tribes were eager to invade Byzantine lands.

Before taking on these outside problems, Heraclius knew he had to tighten things up at home. Only with strength and discipline would the Byzantines be able to defeat two such threatening enemies at once.

Changes. Earlier emperors had kept military and civilian matters separate, but now Heraclius decided to reorganize the government by putting local administrations under military rule. He divided the empire's territory into *themes* (also the name for military units), each headed by a *strategos,* or general, instead of a civilian governor. The *strategos* would command both the local government and the local division of the army. In putting everything under military control, Heraclius hoped that decisions could be made more quickly and efficiently. Heraclius also made other changes. For example, he decided that Greek, the region's spoken language, should be the language of government, instead of the traditional Latin. From now on the emperor would be called *basileus,* a Greek word replacing the Latin *augustus.*

Confronting Persia. Meanwhile, Persia continued to conquer Byzantine territory, capturing the ancient city of Jerusalem in 615 and taking over Egypt in 618. Heraclius almost abandoned Constantinople completely and moved the capital to Carthage, out of Persian range. But at the last minute he was persuaded to stay in Constantinople, promising not to leave if the people themselves would promise to make whatever sacrifices he asked of them. They did promise, and in the struggle that followed both sides kept the bargain.

After twelve years of careful preparation, Heraclius decided in 622 that it was finally time to confront the enemy. For the following six years, he put all his efforts into defeating Persia, winning back the lost territory in a series of brilliant victories. At times, he was forced to deal with other problems, especially the troublesome Avars on the empire's western borders. In June 626, one of the empire's greatest moments of danger, the Avars and Persians combined forces, attacking Constantinople by both sea and land. Yet the city's massive walls held out, and the attackers had to give up.

Single combat. In 628 Heraclius won a decisive victory over the Persians at the battle of Nineveh. The battle raged for eleven straight hours, until finally the Persian general challenged Heraclius to single combat. The first emperor in more than two hundred years to lead his troops into battle personally, Heraclius was broad-chested, with a recognizable mane of curly blond hair. He knew how to inspire his soldiers. Without hesitation (so the story goes), he agreed to the duel. Spurring his battle-horse Dorkon, he charged—and cut off the Persian's head with a single stroke of his sword. The battle began again, and the Byzantines fought until sunset, when they suddenly realized that there were hardly any Persians left. Their victory was complete.

Triumph. About one year later, after refusing to surrender, the Persian king was overthrown by his son, who then accepted a Byzantine peace offer. Persia gave up all the land she had conquered, also returning religious prizes (such as the True Cross, on which Christ had been crucified) taken at the capture of Jerusalem. Heraclius held a great Triumph, Rome's traditional victory parade, through the famous Golden Gate at Constantinople's outer wall.

Religious disputes. Yet even in this hour of victory, Heraclius faced major disputes within the church. Since the time of Constantine, the first Roman emperor to become a Christian, emperors had taken a role in trying to solve disagreements within the church. And as the church had grown, its problems had grown with it. Now they threatened the empire's unity. Most of the disputes had to do with the nature of Jesus Christ, whom Christians believed to be the son of God. But was Christ human, or divine? Both? Neither? The church's official position was that Christ combined both in a mysterious way, as one single being who was somehow both completely human and completely divine.

Monophysites. This rather complicated answer wasn't good enough for some, and during the fifth century, one group of Christians had begun claiming that Christ had only a single, divine nature. They were called "monophysites," from the Greek for "single nature." By Heraclius's time this belief had become especially

Welcome Conquerors

The monophysites' disagreements with the empire meant that when the Arabs arrived in places like Syria and Egypt, local Christians sometimes welcomed them as a relief from Byzantine rule. In contrast to the Byzantines, the Muslim Arabs let the local Christians continue to worship as they pleased. Original Christian populations still survive in such areas, for example, in Egypt, where they are called Copts. In the long run, though, the majority have become Muslims, either through Arab immigration or through the Christians' converting to Islam.

▲ Heraclius humbly carries the relic of the True Cross through Constantinople's Golden Gate.

popular in parts of the Middle East, including Syria, Palestine, and Egypt. The local peoples there did not always like being under Byzantine rule, and they saw the official church as being part of the government. Having their own religious beliefs was also a way for them to express their desire for independence from the empire.

Islam. While Heraclius tried to heal these conflicts in his church and empire, a new and powerful religious force was gathering strength deep in the deserts of Arabia. Called Islam, it was founded by an Arab named **Muhammad** (see entry). Before becoming Muslims, as Islam's followers are called, the nomadic Arabic tribes had always been independent and often at war with each other. During his lifetime, however, Muhammad and his message unified them. And after Muhammad's death in 632, his successors, called the caliphs, led the Arabs on a remarkable campaign of conquest. With the enthusiasm and confidence of those who believe they are backed by a powerful god, the Arabs burst out of the desert in 633. Their first target was Byzantine-controlled Syria and Palestine. Their attack came as a complete surprise.

Battle of Yarmuk. As the Arabs invaded from the south, Heraclius was in the city of Antioch, in the northern part of Syria. With the defeat of Persia under his belt, he was now at the height of his reputation. Yet the empire was exhausted from generations of war. The Arabs easily occupied southern Syria and Palestine, capturing the major city of Damascus and attacking Jerusalem. Once he heard of the invasion, it took Heraclius over a year to raise an army big enough to confront the Arabs. In the meantime, smaller Byzantine forces sent out to test the opposition were completely destroyed.

Culture Clashes

Centered in Constantinople, the Byzantine heartland—today's Greece and Turkey—was a Greek-speaking area. Elsewhere in the eastern Mediterranean, in places such as Syria and Egypt, only the ruling classes spoke Greek. Local people spoke their own languages and had their own cultures. Along with religious issues, such cultural differences made it easier for local people to turn their backs on Byzantium and welcome Islam.

The Byzantine army was finally ready in 636. Amounting to some eighty thousand men, it was placed under the command of Heraclius's brother, Theodore. It marched south and for three months camped near the Arab position on the Yarmuk River. Though they outnumbered the Arabs, the Byzantines did not attack. Their hesitation proved costly. Arab reinforcements arrived. Soon after, a sandstorm arose that blew right in the Byzantines' faces. Under its cover, the Arabs attacked and totally wiped out the unprepared Byzantine army.

Collapse. The defeat at Yarmuk shattered the Byzantines' spirits. From then on, Heraclius seemed to lose his old energy. He fell ill soon after, both physically and mentally, suffering from a painful disease of the body and developing an irrational fear of the sea. During his last years, he was little more than a feeble shadow of the warrior-emperor who had led his victorious troops against the Persians. After five years of illness, Heraclius died on February 11, 641.

Further Arab conquests. As for the Persians, they too fell victim to Arab conquests. Soon after Yarmuk, the Arabs defeated the Persians at the battle of Cadesia. And soon after that, they easily conquered the Byzantine province of Egypt. In coming centuries, Islam would replace the Persians as the Byzantine Empire's biggest enemy. While the Byzantines had kept the heartland of their empire, however, the Persians were completely conquered by the Arabs. In conquering these lands, Islam itself was deeply influenced by Byzantine and Persian traditions as it grew into a world culture.

For More Information

Jenkins, Romilly. *Byzantium: The Imperial Centuries, A.D. 610-1071.* Toronto: University of Toronto Press, 1987.

Kaegi, Walter F. *Byzantium and the Early Islamic Conquests.* Cambridge, England: Cambridge University Press, 1992.

Norwich, John Julius. *Byzantium: The Early Centuries.* London: Penguin, 1990.

Punishment?

It was said that Heraclius's illnesses were God's punishment for his sins. For after Eudocia's death in 612, Heraclius had married his own niece, Martina, a union viewed as unlucky by his superstitious subjects and sinful by the church. Several of their children suffered from deformities, though the oldest, Heraclonas, did not. During their father's illness, Heraclonas shared the throne with his half-brother, Constantine, Heraclius's son by Eudocia.

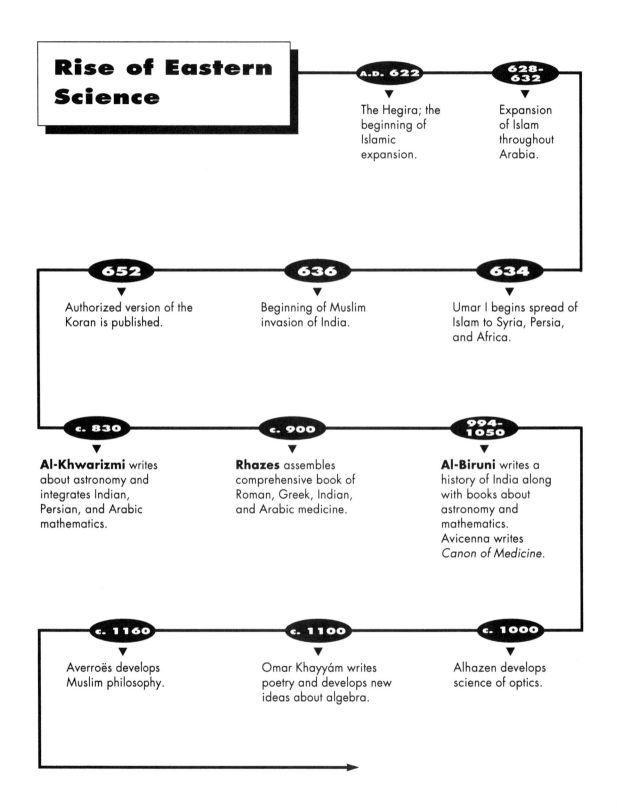

Rise of Eastern Science

A.D. 622
The Hegira; the beginning of Islamic expansion.

628-632
Expansion of Islam throughout Arabia.

652
Authorized version of the Koran is published.

636
Beginning of Muslim invasion of India.

634
Umar I begins spread of Islam to Syria, Persia, and Africa.

c. 830
Al-Khwarizmi writes about astronomy and integrates Indian, Persian, and Arabic mathematics.

c. 900
Rhazes assembles comprehensive book of Roman, Greek, Indian, and Arabic medicine.

994-1050
Al-Biruni writes a history of India along with books about astronomy and mathematics. Avicenna writes *Canon of Medicine*.

c. 1160
Averroës develops Muslim philosophy.

c. 1100
Omar Khayyám writes poetry and develops new ideas about algebra.

c. 1000
Alhazen develops science of optics.

RISE OF
EASTERN
SCIENCE

The year 622 marked the beginning of one of the greatest military expansions in world history. Following his flight from Mecca to Medina, the prophet of Islam, Muhammad, quickly spread a new religion across the Arabian desert, unifying the diverse nomadic tribes first through religion and then through a common language and a commitment to crusade. Armed with a new religious word that would later become the Koran as well as sword and camel, the fighting nomads came together to sweep north into Syria and Persia and west across northern Africa. In less than two hundred years, the army of Islam had conquered land from northern India to Spain. The Arabic language became the language of the conquered nations, and Islam became the dominant religion in Africa and the Middle East.

The militant Arabs had long roamed a vast desert wilderness, little touched by outside influences. The rapid expansion brought the warriors into contact with the whole history of knowledge gathered in Europe and India. The Muslims, as the followers of Islam are called, now centrally located between the ancient cultures of Europe and Asia, were quick to recognize the opportunity to add to their own wisdom. Muslim rulers brought Byzantine and Indian wise men to their courts and sent Muslim scholars to distant countries in search of knowledge.

The new religion, Islam, encouraged an explosion of knowledge as rapid as the military expansion. It became, for example, a religious necessity to determine the exact locations of major cities and the exact times for prayer in each location. Muslim scholars gathered astronomical and mathematical information and technology to add to their own—a step that greatly increased the world's knowledge in these areas. Their adaptation of the Indian number system gave the Western world an "Arabic" number system vastly more simple to use than the earlier Greek or Roman systems.

The initial Islamic thirst for knowledge encouraged Muslim rulers of even the smallest provinces to sponsor the studies of scholars. Such instruments as the astrolabe, a tool for measuring positions of stars and planets, and diverse areas of study such as algebra and literature developed greatly under the sponsorship of these rulers. One of the sponsored scholars was **al-Khwarizmi,** a student and prolific writer of books about mathematics and astronomy. He is credited with bringing the Hindu number system, with its decimal notation, to the West. Another sponsored scholar, **al-Biruni,** studied and wrote about circles and chords, time, longitude and latitude, locations, the sextant, and the astrolabe—always with a commentary on the sources of his information and the reliability of other scholars. Perhaps his greatest contribution was in acquainting the West with the history and culture of the East. One of his most lasting works was a book about the history and people of India.

Perhaps the greatest advancements, however, were in the field of medicine. Arab scholars translated Eastern and Western medical journals and applied their own experiences to bring together the medical knowledge of the entire known world. In Baghdad, the capital of the Muslim world, **Rhazes,** a medical scholar who was head of Baghdad's hospital, spent many years assembling Eastern and Western medical ideas and testing them against his own experiences. Thus Rhazes helped to break the hold of ancient physicians such as Galen and revive medical studies. He carefully described common diseases and their symptoms and gave the world new medical tools for setting broken bones and for use in surgery.

▲ **Arab astronomers; Islam encouraged an explosion of knowledge.**

The search for knowledge in the Islamic world continued for several hundred years. In the eleventh century, for example, scholars such as Alhazen expanded Islamic interest into other areas of study. Alhazen revolutionized the study of light and sight. And in the twelfth century, Omar Khayyám added much to the world's knowledge of algebra while contributing to a growing body of Arabic literature with his enduring *Rubáiyat,* or "Arabian Nights." In that same century, the Spanish-Arabian philosopher Averroës began to try to relate the faith of Islam to ideas of reason, a project continued for the Jewish religion by Moses Maimonides and for the Christians by St. Thomas Aquinas.

The rapid expansion of knowledge that accompanied the introduction of Islam gave rise to the tremendous growth of Arabic literature and science through the fourteenth century, keeping alive the search for knowledge through a period of decline of Western scholarliness.

Rhazes

c. 865-between 923 and 935

Personal Background

A little-known public figure. Historians can piece together a picture of Rhazes (Abu Bakr Muhammad ibn Zakariya ar-Razi; commonly known as ar-Razi) from his own writings and from the writings of his critics. Although he was a doctor and hospital director, Rhazes found time to write more than two hundred books and articles. But these are scholarly writings, not autobiographical ones, so we do not know what he looked like or how he received enough education to enter medical school. Historians are certain, however, that Rhazes was a real person, or in the language of historians, "a historical figure."

Rhazes was born in the city of Rayy (near present-day Tehran, Iran) in about 865. While not much is known about his early life, it is certain that he grew up to have very strong opinions about nearly everything that people were debating in his time.

Physician. When he had received enough education in his own home town, Rhazes, as a young man, traveled to Baghdad to attend medical school. Here he became acquainted with the ideas of Western medicine—he learned about the Greek physician Galen, who had practiced medicine in Rome in the second century A.D., and about the Greek philosopher Aristotle, who had lived 1300 years before Rhazes, in the fourth century B.C.

▲ In Baghdad, the capital of the Muslim world, Rhazes gathered medical information from the West and East and integrated it with his own observations.

Event: Developing Islamic medicine.

Role: Born in a small city in Persia, Rhazes moved from his native district to study medicine in Baghdad. There he became not only a physician but also a philosopher and writer. His many writings reflect forward thinking in many fields. His *Comprehensive Book* was used as a medical textbook for centuries.

When Rhazes finished medical school, he returned home to Rayy and soon became director of the hospital there. Apparently, the job as hospital director was not too time consuming: Rhazes found a great deal of time to write, and he wrote about many subjects. He was not particularly fond of organized religions, so he wrote books about how people should behave without religion. Two of these books, translated as "The Book of Spiritual Physick" and "The Philosopher's Way of Life," have been published in Western languages. These are just two of many writings that illustrate how Rhazes disagreed with other learned men of his time. Because his opponents also wrote what they thought about Rhazes' ideas, his positions on many issues of his day are well known.

Some of Rhazes' ideas. One of the practices of the day that Rhazes disagreed with was that people of similar intelligence should be grouped together in separate levels of society, much as students today are sometimes grouped together in the same classes according to their perceived abilities. Rhazes, however, believed that everyone was equal and had an equal measure of ability. Thus, he thought, everyone had the ability to make decisions and to deal with day-to-day matters for themselves. Furthermore, Rhazes held that the ideas of the average person of any occupation were just as worthy of investigation as the ideas of the supposedly learned men.

Islamic writers of the tenth century believed that human societies were formed under the directions of prophets. Rhazes, though, apparently didn't believe in prophets. His book *The Tricks of the Prophets* discussed the miracles of the prophets, which, it seems, Rhazes didn't believe were miracles at all. His exact opinions on the matter, however, were lost with the book's manuscript.

Rhazes generally rejected mystical or magical explanations for scientific events. He studied alchemy, an ancient science that attempted to change one type of material into another. It was, in Rhazes' time, considered to be more mystical than scientific in nature (although alchemy later laid the foundation for the modern science of chemistry). Rhazes tried to approach alchemy scientifically, giving exact accounts of the materials used and what happened to them. That led him to believe in a sort of small-particle construction of matter (like atoms). However, he later agreed with others of his day that the five elements, earth, water, air, fire, and ether (a heavenly element), were the ingredients from which all material things are formed, not small particles like atoms.

In the sciences, too, Rhazes was often at odds with the leading thinkers of his day. Because most astronomers and mathematicians of the 900s studied time by marking the movements of objects in the skies, they thought that time wouldn't exist unless the heavenly bodies moved. Rhazes believed that time would continue even if all the stars, planets, and moons stopped moving. In fact, he wrote, there were some things that existed before the earth was formed: a creator, a soul, matter, time, and space.

In Rhazes' own field of medicine, most doctors of his time believed that common diseases occurred just as Galen had described them. But Rhazes believed that he had seen evidence that contradicted Galen's observations. In his book *Concerns about Galen,* Rhazes urged practicing doctors to continue to make their own observations and judgments about illnesses and not to rely only on Galen's ideas.

Enemies. Because of all his disagreements with commonly held ideas, many people of his time were unhappy with Rhazes. They accused him of corrupting their souls and destroying their bodies. Mostly they seemed to be worried about Rhazes' own soul, since he seemed not to believe in prophets. Rhazes spent much of his time on the move, avoiding politicians who might not agree with him. For a time, he was director of the larger hospital at Baghdad. But then political winds sent him back to Rayy. It was a pattern that would be repeated throughout his adult life. Still, he was never threatened or imprisoned for his ideas.

The opportunities of Islam. It had been three hundred years since Muhammad had begun to spread a new religion from Arabia with book and sword. Islamic soldier-missionaries had spread their religion across the Arab peninsula, then north through Persia and east into India. These soldiers also moved west to challenge the old Byzantine Empire and to unite the people of north Africa. The strength of Islam brought more peace to the region and stirred a new exchange of ideas between East and

West. Rhazes collected these ideas, particularly about medicine, and spent much of his time adding his own thoughts and writing about the world's knowledge. In all, Rhazes is supposed to have written 128 large books and 28 small ones, 12 about chemistry alone, along with many articles and pamphlets.

Participation: Developing Islamic Medicine

The legacy of Rhazes. Anyone who has had a broken arm or leg, or has been placed in a cast while some body part heals, has benefitted from the work of Rhazes the physician. It was Rhazes who invented the use of plaster of Paris to make strong casts. And in the field of surgery, Rhazes originated the idea of sewing up wounds with thread drawn from the guts of animals—an idea that sped healing.

Mostly, however, Rhazes influenced modern medicine by recording his careful observations of life-threatening diseases. One of his books was devoted to describing the symptoms and remedies of two terrible diseases of his day, smallpox and measles.

Comprehensive Book. Combining ideas from Greece, Syria, Persia, and India with his own observations, Rhazes wrote his greatest medical book, titled *al-Hawi,* or the *Comprehensive Book.* It was an attempt to describe the symptoms and treatments for nearly all the diseases known at that time. The most complete assembly of medical information available at that time, the completed "book" was really a ten-volume encyclopedia of medicine.

Rhazes' medical knowledge reached for ideas far beyond his time. Six hundred years before Louis Pasteur cited germs as being causes of disease, Rhazes, for example, wrote about the role of germs in meat spoilage. However, because Rhazes wrote in Ara-

Some Subjects of Rhazes' Books

Ethics
The Book of Spiritual Physick
The Philosopher's Way of Life

Cosmology
The Divine Science

Religion
The Tricks of the Prophets

Medicine
On Smallpox and Measles
Comprehensive Book

bic, it took many years for the valuable information in the *Comprehensive Book* to reach the West.

Aftermath

Opposition to Rhazes' ideas. Another obstacle to the spread of Rhazes' ideas was the opposition of other famous medical men who thought themselves philosophers. A great Muslim philosopher, Avicenna (also known as Ibn Sina), who flourished seventy years after Rhazes died, thought that Rhazes should have stayed with medicine and that even in this subject he did not have the intelligence to do more than deal with boils and urine. The great fifteenth-century Jewish philosopher-physician from Spain, Moses Maimonides, rejected Rhazes' ideas on religion and ethics completely. He was after all, Maimonides thought, only a physician.

Spreading popularity. It was some time before the *Comprehensive Book* was translated into a Western language. A Jewish doctor, Faraj ben-Salim, translated it into Greek in 1279. From that time, it became a well-used textbook in Western medical schools. The book's popularity took it into several editions in the West, where in 1542 it reached its fifth Western edition in Venice, Italy, and in the East, where it was translated into Hindi.

In the last few years of his life, Rhazes retired to a quiet and comfortable life in Rayy. His study of medicine in his own hospital and his knowledge of medical practices in other countries had made him one of the world's greatest medical authorities.

For More Information

Hitti, Philip. *History of the Arabs.* New York: St. Martin's, 1964.
Lewis, Bernard. *The Arabs in History.* New York: Harper and Row, 1960.

Al-Khwarizmi

c. 783-c. 850

Personal Background

Early Life. Abu Ja'Far Muhammad ibn Musa al-Khwarizmi's name indicates that he was born in Khwarezm, an ancient state in the khanate of Khiva, situated on the lower Amu Darya, a river in today's Uzbekistan. In Persian and Arabic names the prefix "al-" means "from," and the word that follows is often the name of the town in which a person was born. However, Al-Tabari, a famous Persian historian who was writing just after Khwarizmi died, gave him another name, al-Qutrubbulli. It is likely that Khwarizmi's ancestors came from Uzbekistan, but that the great astronomer and mathematician was actually born at Qutrubbulli, a little south of the Muslim capital of Baghdad, in present-day Iraq. Little is known about al-Khwarizmi's childhood or education.

What is certain, however, is that al-Khwarizmi was well educated. He was one of the wise men brought to Baghdad about 815 by the ruling Abbaside family, who had overthrown the old line of Persian rulers in 750. Soon after, the Abbasides moved the Muslim capital from Damascus, a city glittering with golden domes and colorful tile that was a seat of learning and Islamic religion, to Baghdad, beginning a period historian/soldier Sir John Glubb called "the age of wealth and culture" (Glubb, p. 98).

▲ A page from an Islamic treatise on cosmology; al-Khwarizmi used a water clock and an astrolabe to create a table of movements of planets and stars.

Event: Bringing Eastern mathematics and astronomy to the West.

Role: Living at a time often referred to as the Muslim age of wealth and culture, al-Khwarizmi was a noted mathematician and astronomer who gathered—and built upon—important scientific ideas of his day. He wrote numerous books on algebra, astronomy, and other topics, thereby expanding upon and preserving knowledge for future generations.

Participation:
Bringing Eastern Mathematics
and Astronomy to the West

The age of wealth and culture. In 813 Caliph Mamoon ruled Persia, and he emphasized the importance of learning. He brought together the greatest scholars in his realm and formed them into his House of Wisdom and supported their studies—studies always within the rules of Islam. One of the learned men called to Baghdad was al-Khwarizmi.

Europe and Asia. At the time al-Khwarizmi came to Baghdad to study astronomy and mathematics, those subjects had already been studied in Asia and in Europe for many years. Chinese people had had a sound calendar for nearly two thousand years, which meant they knew something about the movements of the sun, moon, and planets. Six hundred years earlier the famous astronomer Ptolemy had begun to find ways to chart the heavens. Although he mistakenly placed the earth at the center of the universe, Ptolemy's books were still being used when al-Khwarizmi took up his studies. On the other side of Persia, Hindu scholars in India had developed their own ideas on astronomy and some simple tools to study the stars and planets. The Hindus had also developed a number system that was much more efficient than the previous system, which had used letters to represent 1, 10, 20, 30, etc. Al-Khwarizmi had an opportunity to study Ptolemy, Hindu mathematics, and the work of Greek astronomers. He gathered all this information and added his own ideas, thereby uniting Eastern and Western ideas about astronomy and mathematics.

Writing about algebra. Al-Khwarizmi must have been a very practical man. His first book is now called *Algebra,* short for *Al-Kitab al-mukhtasar fi hisab al-jabr wa'l-muqabala* ("The Compendious Book on Calculation by Completion and Balancing"). In it he tried to provide "what is easiest and most useful in arithmetic, such as men constantly require in cases of inheritance, legacies, partition, lawsuits, and trade, and in all their dealings with one another" (Al-Khwarizmi in Rosen, p. 3).

The first part of *Algebra* contains about eight hundred examples of simple algebra problems. He explains how to get rid of minus signs by adding the same amount to each side of the equation (completion) and then collecting terms so that all like terms lie on one side of the equation (balancing). Apparently al-Khwarizmi was not familiar with or did not like the Greek method of using letters to name values such as 1, 10, 20, 30, etc., so all his explanations are written out in words. For example, one of his explanations begins:

> A quantity: I multiplied a third of it and a dirham by a fourth of it and a dirham; it becomes twenty. Its computation is that you multiply a third of something by a fourth of something: it comes to a half of a sixth of a square. (*Dictionary of Scientific Biography,* p. 359)

That is the first step in solving an equation that would now be written as $(1/3x + 1)(x/4 + 1) = 20$. It is interesting to note that today we write in shorthand such as this partly because al-Khwarizmi's longhand methods were too cumbersome. In *Algebra* he goes on to deal with business mathematics and with measuring, giving all examples as long word problems.

Astronomy and religion. The tools al-Khwarizmi used for his study of astronomy were ancient ones—a water clock and an astrolabe, which he improved upon. He used these to create a table of the movements of planets and stars. Earlier tables had been made, the most popular one in the West by Ptolemy five hundred years before al-Khwarizmi's time.

Al-Khwarizmi applied this new-found knowledge to his religion. Because Muslims marked the beginning of a month by the appearance of a new moon, al-Khwarizmi decided to find out exactly when to expect a new moon. He measured the angle

Some Books by al-Khwarizmi

Subject
Book

Algebra
Al-Kitab al-mukhtasar fi hisab al-jabr wa'l-muqabala

Astrolabe
Kitab 'amal al-asturlab (title translated as "Book on the Construction of the Astrolabe")

Kitab aal'amal bi'l-asturlab ("Book on the Operation of the Astrolabe")

Astrology (published in 826)
Kitab al-ta'rikh

Astronomy tables (832)
Zif al-sindhind

Geography (816)
Kitab surat al-ard ("Book of the Form of the Earth")

Jewish calendar
Isikhraj ta'rikh al-yahud ("Extraction of the Jewish Era")

between the earth, moon, and sun and found that the new moon made its first appearance when lines from the earth (at Baghdad) to the sun and moon marked an angle of twelve degrees. He also used his skills to help him remember when to pray. Muslims were supposed to pray five times every day at very specific times. His practical mind led him to make a simple tool for marking prayer times. It was a flat surface two feet long. On one end stood a pole (now called a gnomon) twelve inches high. Watching the shadow of the pole on the surface, al-Khwarizmi could match it with his water clock time and mark the prayer times.

The shadow was different in various places in his world, of course, but al-Khwarizmi's interest in another subject—geography—would help with that problem. Another book of his listed the longitude and latitude of cities and towns, the centers of seas, islands, mountains, and places along rivers.

Borrowing from India. With all this study of astronomy, geography, and business that required solving arithmetic problems, al-Khwarizmi must have grown weary of writing problems out in words, or of using Roman numerals or Greek letters while solving problems. Whatever his reason, sometime during the 830s, al-Khwarizmi wrote a book about the numbering system used by the people of India. They had devised a system that used symbols that were easy to manipulate in arithmetic problems. When they counted they simply wrote numerals for 1, 2, 3, 4, 5, etc., as is done today. Al-Khwarizmi seems to have been the first to call this system to the attention of the people of the West and Middle East.

Aftermath

Al-Khwarizmi did not make many great discoveries of his own. The branch of mathematics that his name is attached to, algebra, was already developed further than his book explored. The Hindus were already using a simple system of numerals. Romans, Greeks, and Egyptians had already developed effective ways of measuring such things as land and lakes. His work on the mathematics of sines used a base of 150 when the Western world had already adopted a base of 60. Still, he is recognized as one of the great ancient scientists, whose skill lay in bringing together the best or most useful knowledge from all corners of the known world.

Algebra becomes a textbook. In 833 al-Khwarizmi's patron, Caliph Mamoon, died, and the great age of Muslim science began to fade. Some of the original writing of al-Khwarizmi was lost, only to be rediscovered and reprinted in Latin by the Romans. After Al-Khwarizmi's death, *Algebra* was translated and used as a college textbook to teach beginning algebra. It would be a standard textbook in Western universities until the twelfth century.

Al-Khwarizmi's book on Hindu numerals was also translated into Western languages. The system of numerals was adopted by Western mathematicians, who preferred to give credit to al-Khwarizmi rather than to the Hindu inventors. These number tags are now called Arabic numerals.

Charting the Earth

Before al-Khwarizmi's time, the Western authority on the shape of the earth was the second century A.D. astronomer Ptolemy. Ptolemy thought the Mediterranean Sea was much larger than it really is. Al-Khwarizmi calculated this sea to be only five-sixths the size Ptolemy had proposed. Later geographers with better tools found the real size to be even smaller. However, Ptolemy and al-Khwarizmi agreed on at least one thing: both thought, incorrectly, that the Atlantic Ocean was an inland ocean, a very large lake.

For More Information

Dictionary of Scientific Biography. New York: McGraw Hill, 1970.

Glubb, John. *The Great Arab Conquests.* Englewood Cliffs, New Jersey: Prentice-Hall, 1964.

Goldstein, Bernard R. *Ibn al-Muthanna's Commentary on the Astronomical Tables of al-Khwarizmi.* New Haven, Connecticut: Yale University Press, 1967.

Hitti, Philip K. *History of the Arabs.* 8th edition. London: Macmillan, 1964.

King, David A. *Al-Khwarizmi and New Trends in Mathematical Astronomy in the Ninth Century,* Occasional Papers on the Near East, No. 2. New York: New York University, Hagop Kevorkian Center for Near Eastern Studies, 1983.

Neugebauer, O. *The Astronomical Tables of al-Khwarizmi.* Historisk-filosofiske Skrifter, Vol. 4, No. 2. Copenhagen: Ejnar Munksgaard, 1962.

Rosen, Frederic, editor and translator. *The Algebra of Mohammad ben Musa.* New York: G. Olms, Lubrecht and Cramer, 1986.

Al-Biruni

973-1048

Personal Background

Abu ar-Rayhan Muhammad ibn Ahmad al-Biruni, or al-Biruni, as he is known in Western writing, was born in Khwarezm, a region south of the Aral Sea, in a town on the bank of the Amu Darya in what is now Uzbekistan. The actual town in which he was born is now named after the famous historian. Little is known about al-Biruni's early life, except that he spent his early days in the two main cities of Khwarezm, Kath and Jurjaniyya. He was born of Iranian parents, and he once claimed that he did not even know his own father, although that statement is doubtful. His family must have been reasonably well-off, however, because al-Biruni began to study astronomy at an early age under a well-known astronomer and mathematician, Abu Nasr Mansur.

By the age of seventeen, al-Biruni had begun to make his own observations of the sun. He even created a tool—a large ring marked off in halves of one degree—to measure the sun's position in the sky. After four years, he expanded this ring to be fifteen cubits in diameter (a cubit was the length of an arm from the tip of the middle finger to the elbow). He was prepared to use his tool to make more accurate measurements of the sun but had the chance to use it only once before civil war in the region forced him to leave.

Political turmoil. Al-Biruni lived at a time when the spread of Islam had created a thirst for knowledge and had made it possi-

▲ **An Islamic scholar; al-Biruni lived at a time when new ideas from all corners of the known world were being brought together.**

Event: Performing an in-depth study of Indian culture.

Role: Al-Biruni was an astronomer and historian who is best known for his comprehensive book on Indian culture, *The History of India*. Born of Iranian parents, he studied and taught in India and later spent much of his life in Afghanistan. He was a prolific writer, and his many travel books provided readers with views and histories of many different countries.

ble to bring together new ideas from all corners of the known world. "For the first time in history, science became international on a large scale," observed one writer (Hourani, p. 77). It was also an age of rapid political change. The days of complete control by a single Muslim caliph had gone. Large family dynasties had arisen and fallen apart. Samanids had for a time controlled much of present-day Afghanistan and Iran, and the Buwayhids ruled over lands between the Caspian Sea and the Persian Gulf. In al-Biruni's time these dynasties were rapidly giving way to the Ghaznavids, whose capital was at Ghazna in Afghanistan. Over all this area, the shadowy caliph in Baghdad, much like some of the early popes, held some influence bought by handling coronations and sealing government rights with the blessings of Islam.

Khwarezmian

The people of Khwarezm used an Iranian language of their own called Khwarezmian. Al-Biruni thought that finding scientific literature in that language would be as odd as seeing a camel on a roof gutter (*Dictionary of Scientific Biography,* vol. 2, p. 155). As a young astronomer, al-Biruni learned Arabic and Persian. He could also read some Greek, Hebrew, and the Syrian language. Later he learned Sanskrit.

Minor princes vied for control of lands, which resulted in numerous political squabbles. They also competed with each other for knowledge. Superior scholars were sought and supported by the local rulers. Al-Biruni himself had enjoyed the protection of his local ruler. In 995, however, the lord of Kath, who ruled over the area, was attacked and killed by the emir (ruler) of Jurjaniyya. Al-Biruni went into hiding and then left the country. His whereabouts after that are uncertain, though he may have wandered to the city of Rayy, made famous by the great hospital director **Rhazes** (see entry). At least he later said that he was there in miserable conditions; without a sponsor, al-Biruni was forced to support himself.

Finding a sponsor. Al-Biruni was able to return in about 997 to Kath, where his studies began to pay dividends. He wrote about his observations of a lunar eclipse in a cooperative effort with another astronomer in Baghdad. Sharing their observations, they were able to determine the difference in longitude between the two cities. About this time, the remains of the Samanid dynasty were ruled by Mansur II, who became al-Biruni's first royal sponsor. Al-Biruni later wrote a bit of poetry that hinted that he once lived in Mansur's court at Bukhara.

Al-Biruni had not long to work for Mansur, however, before another prince arrived in the area. Qabus had been driven out of his own land and had come to Bukhara seeking help. When he succeeded in regaining his power, he took al-Biruni with him to his capital at Gurgan. About the year 1000, al-Biruni wrote one of his most famous works, *Chronology,* and dedicated it to his sponsor, Qabus.

Al-Biruni wanted to establish a great astronomy center in the desert east of the Caspian Sea to measure such things as degrees of longitude. Qabus was apparently not interested, so by the year 1004 al-Biruni had gone to the city of Jurjaniyya in his homeland. There he was sponsored by Abu' `Abbas Ma'mun, who held the title Khwarezmshah—Shah of Khwarezm. With the shah's financial support, al-Biruni was now able to build his tools for measuring distances and movements in the heavens.

A tongue of silver. The shah was soon caught in a power play between two rulers, the caliph Qadir and the prince Mahmud, who was Ma'mun's overlord. Mahmud wanted his name to be included in the Friday prayers of the local Muslims. Ma'mun was afraid to do this because his own advisers opposed it and the caliph would certainly be offended. The local chiefs were particularly opposed. Al-Biruni was known for his ability as a convincing speaker, so he was sent to calm the chiefs. But Ma'mun, meanwhile, undercut al-Biruni's efforts by putting Mahmud's name in prayers. Outraged, the chiefs rose up and killed Ma'mun. Mahmud then invaded Ma'mun's domain with an army and took charge of the whole region. Al-Biruni was again without a sponsor and was carried away by Mahmud because of his efforts with the chiefs.

Al-Biruni ended up in Kabul, Afghanistan, where he continued to study and write about astronomy, but now with very poor instruments. Al-Biruni complained that he was treated cruelly and without respect by his new lord. Nevertheless, Mahmud did finance the astronomer enough so that al-Biruni called his new observation ring the Yamini ring, after the title the caliph had been given, Sultan Mahmud-Yamin al-Dawla, "Right Hand of the State." Al-Biruni also profited by Mahmud's greed. The sultan continually expanded his territory by conquest until he controlled part of present-day India. Al-Biruni then had the opportunity to travel and study in India.

Participation: Performing an In-depth Study of Indian Culture

Living in India. Al-Biruni lived and studied in the Punjab and Kashmir regions of India for about eight years. He learned the Indian language, Sanskrit, and was able to compare his own astronomy with the work that had been done in India. For part of this time, he stayed at Nandana Fort, which was taken by Mahmud as a base for excursions into the Indus Valley.

Nandana Fort

The old Nandana fort that became a home for al-Biruni was near the place where Macedonian conqueror Alexander the Great had taken his elephants and soldiers across the Jhelum River on his way to the Indus Valley. Later, the Moghuls (certain Indian Muslims) would use the same route in their invasion of India.

A prolific writer. From the age of seventeen or eighteen, al-Biruni wrote extensively. He liked to compare his own observations with those of other people, and he gathered information about a great many subjects. He wrote at least 146 major books, averaging ninety pages each, on such subjects as astronomy, astrology, time, geography, arithmetic, geometry, trigonometry, mechanics, meteorology, gems, religion, and magic. His book on pharmacology contains a detailed listing of 760 drugs, describing their origins and uses. Along the way he also wrote stories and poems to fill sixteen books.

The titles of al-Biruni's books are deceiving, for he rarely stayed with his original subject. More often than not, he interrupted himself with comments about other scholars, or descriptions of religions, or his own complaints about how the world had treated him. A book about time, for example, begins with a description of a day, lunar month, and year, then moves to the calendars of Jews, Assyrians, Babylonians, and Persians. The same book also tells about plants and the various religions al-Biruni encountered, as well as about the festivals and feasts of the peoples of the Middle East. Very often, his books explain a subject from the point of view of people in other countries.

Al-Biruni seems to have been a "how-to" writer as well. He wrote directions for making and using an astrolabe and a sextant, measuring a degree of longitude, making astrological forecasts, and solving problems dealing with astronomy. In most of these books he did not hesitate to call attention to his own discoveries or his own work. When he was sixty-three, for example, he wrote a book listing all the known writings of the famous physician Rhazes. But he managed to include a list of the books he had written himself by that time, 113 of them.

Tahqiq ma li'l-Hind. In what is one of his greatest books, al-Biruni introduced the people and customs of India to the Muslims. While he was in India, al-Biruni began a most complete study of the Indian culture. Published as *Tahqiq ma li'l-Hind* ("The History of India") it began with an explanation of the difficulties he encountered in his studies: the Sanskrit language was difficult to learn; Indians were very different from non-Indians and therefore were hard to understand; and Indians distrusted foreign questioners.

Religion

Al-Biruni was a stalwart Muslim, although whether he was of the Shiite or Sunni sects cannot be told from his writing. Sometimes he writes as if holding Shiite traditions sacred and sometimes his religious convictions seem to be Sunni, perhaps because he changed sponsors from time to time and some of them were Shiite and some Sunni. He even cautiously seemed to like the ideas of Christianity, saying "Upon my life, this is a noble philosophy, but the people of the world are not all philosophers." (al-Biruni in Sachau, vol. 2, p. 161)

Though he was determined to tell in "The History of India" only what he saw and heard personally, al-Biruni nevertheless could not resist drawing comparisons between Indian and Greek customs wherever possible. And he found that the Greeks and the Indians had much in common. For example, the common people of both countries worshiped idols, while the wealthy concentrated on a single god of their family. For this reason, al-Biruni thought the wealthy might be easily led along the Muslim way. "Those who follow the way of salvation or the path of reason and argument, and who want the truth, would avoid worshiping anyone except God alone," he wrote (Hourani, p. 54).

▲ An Arabian astrolabe, circa 1014; al-Biruni wrote directions for
making and using an astrolabe and a sextant, among other things.

The bulk of "The History of India"'s more than sixty-five chap-
ters provides a look into many aspects of Indian culture, including
religions, God, the soul, marriage, literature, writing, rules of
chess, ideas about time, the number system, calendars, pilgrim-
ages, diets, lawsuits, festivals, and astrological measurements and
cycles. The book was one of the earliest and most serious attempts
at bringing the knowledge and ideas of India to the Muslim world.
It was major step in the great Muslim search for and assembly of
knowledge that accompanied the rapid Muslim conquests.

A lasting legacy outside of Islam. From the time he was fifty years old until he was sixty-one, al-Biruni suffered from an unknown illness that left him weak and dimmed his eyesight. He continued to work and write with the aid of an assistant. Then at age sixty-one he seemed to recover his strength and began to work vigorously on astronomy, mathematics, and history once more. He became known to the scholars of his time as al-Usicadh, "the Master." He was more tolerant of other societies than many of his contemporaries, setting prayer times using a Byzantine calendar, for example. Nevertheless, his great observations were for a long time lost outside the Muslim world. Only in the late nineteenth century did some of the writings emerge as translations in Western languages. In the medieval West, al-Biruni, one of the world's greatest historians and most careful observers, was lost—only remembered and admired in his own region.

> ## Al-Biruni on Indian Social Classes
>
> One part of Indian culture that distressed al-Biruni was the Indian caste system, which divided people into different social classes and gave some citizens more privileges than others. "The Indians in our time make numerous distinctions among human beings," he noted. "We differ from them in this, for we regard all men as equal except in piety. This is the greatest barrier between them and Islam" (al-Biruni in Sachau, Vol. 1, p. 100).

Al-Biruni died an old man sometime after 1050 at the town known as Ghazni, Afghanistan.

For More Information

Dictionary of Scientific Biography, New York: McGraw Hill, 1970.

Hourani, Albert. *The Story of the Arab Peoples.* Cambridge, Massachusetts: Belknap Press, 1991.

Sachau, E. *Alberuni's India.* 2 vols. London: Sachau, 1888.

Schacht, J., and C. E. Bosworth, editors. *The Legacy of Islam.* Oxford, England: Oxford University Press, 1974.

Viking Invasion of Britain

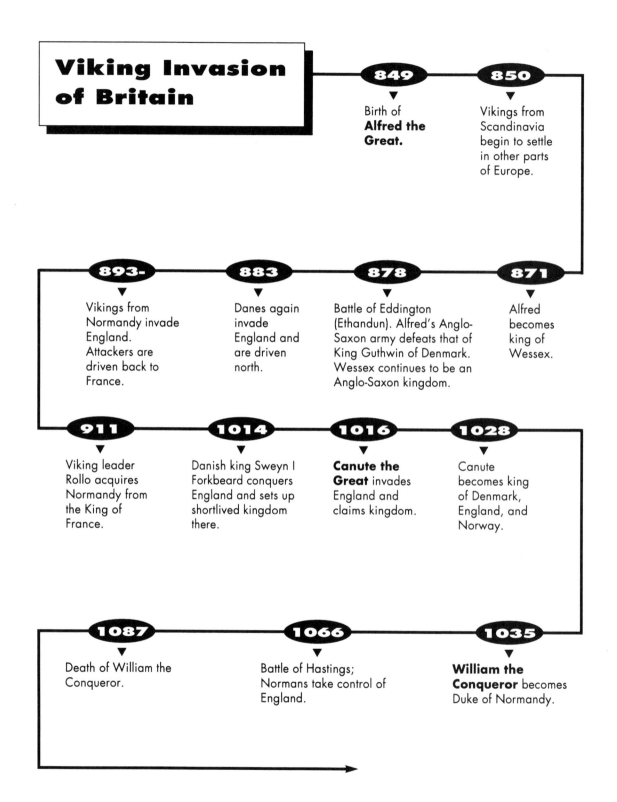

849
▼
Birth of **Alfred the Great.**

850
▼
Vikings from Scandinavia begin to settle in other parts of Europe.

871
▼
Alfred becomes king of Wessex.

878
▼
Battle of Eddington (Ethandun). Alfred's Anglo-Saxon army defeats that of King Guthwin of Denmark. Wessex continues to be an Anglo-Saxon kingdom.

883
▼
Danes again invade England and are driven north.

893-
▼
Vikings from Normandy invade England. Attackers are driven back to France.

911
▼
Viking leader Rollo acquires Normandy from the King of France.

1014
▼
Danish king Sweyn I Forkbeard conquers England and sets up shortlived kingdom there.

1016
▼
Canute the Great invades England and claims kingdom.

1028
▼
Canute becomes king of Denmark, England, and Norway.

1035
▼
William the Conqueror becomes Duke of Normandy.

1066
▼
Battle of Hastings; Normans take control of England.

1087
▼
Death of William the Conqueror.

VIKING INVASION OF BRITAIN

As the eighth century A.D. was coming to a close, Vikings, people from the far north Scandinavian countries, grew restless. For centuries they had gradually moved westward until they found themselves crowded along the fjords of Norway. Perhaps because the land along the fjords was rough and difficult to farm and the Norse who lived there may have outgrown the food supply, the Vikings took to the sea for their livelihood. They were expert shipbuilders and sailors, and they found that they could survive by raiding the coasts of Europe and England.

Viking ships roamed the north Atlantic, stopping at coastal settlements and taking food and wealth. They were a powerful and feared force—as many as 350 of their ships could be seen on a single raiding voyage. First stopping along the coast of present-day Germany and France, by 790 the Vikings had extended their raids into Scotland and England. For forty years Vikings intimidated the small kingdoms of the British Isles, demanding booty from the rulers before withdrawing to their Norwegian and Danish homelands.

About 850, however, the fierce sailors changed from raiding to settling. Viking villages began to spring up along the coast of Scotland, England, and France. Charlemagne, the great Frank unifier of Europe, had died in 814, leaving the Holy Roman Empire divided among his sons. Within twenty-five years the power that might have controlled the Viking invasions had collapsed. Viking raids and efforts to establish settlements grew stronger in both England and France. Of the kings of the English sovereignties, only **Alfred the Great** seemed able to hold off an eventual Viking takeover of the British Isles.

Alfred was king of Wessex, the southwest area of England. He was almost constantly at war with the northmen, and even had to hide from their invasion for one four-month period. But in 878 he gathered a large Anglo-Saxon army and defeated the Danish invader King Guthrum at the Battle of Eddington (Ethandun). Alfred's victory delayed Viking settlement in England for nearly two decades, during which time he was able to strengthen his defenses and initiate government reform in Wessex.

Still Viking raids along the coast of Europe continued and became bolder. By 893 renewed efforts were being made to conquer England, this time from bases along the European coast. At the same time, Vikings were penetrating so far into the weakened France as to frighten the French rulers. One Viking leader, Rollo, traveled up the Seine River, toward Paris. To ward off this threat in 911, the king of France made a deal with Rollo. Rollo promised to leave Paris alone in return for Viking ownership of the French coastal region known as Normandy.

In the early eleventh century two kings from Denmark invaded England from the north. King Sweyn I Forkbeard claimed the island nation for Denmark in 1013 and held it for a short time. Two years later, **Canute the Great** returned to claim English rule and also became king of Denmark and Norway. Soon after his death, however, the island reverted to English rule.

Toward the middle of the eleventh century, a strong Norse leader, **William the Conqueror,** took control of Normandy. After destroying all his competitors for Norman rule, William

▶

Vikings landing on the Normandy coast; the Vikings roamed the north Atlantic, stopping at coastal settlements and taking food and wealth.

▲ One of the earliest detailed maps of Great Britain, drawn about
A.D. 1250.

then turned toward England. Earlier, Harold Godwinsson, one of
those contending for English rule, had made promises to the rising William. On the basis of these promises, William claimed
authority to rule England. Harold, however, had no intention of
honoring the promises, or even of remembering them.

Meanwhile another Harold, king of Denmark, was again preparing to invade England from its bases in the north. While Harold of England was occupied with Harold of Denmark, William was preparing his own invasion of the British Isles. Landing a few miles from the trading port of Hastings, William and his army marched to meet English Harold's army, which had been hurriedly recalled from the North.

On October 14, 1066 a one-day war, the Battle of Hastings, changed England forever. William the Conqueror's decisive victory is described in an early account of the battle:

> The battle commenced on both sides. They fought with ardour, neither giving ground, for a great part of the day. Finding this, William gave a signal to his party, that, by a feigned flight, they should retreat. Through this devise, the close body of the English, opening for the purpose of cutting down the straggling enemy, brought upon itself swift destruction; for the Normans, facing about, attacked them thus disordered, and compelled them to fly. In this manner ... they met an honourable death in avenging their country; nor indeed were they at all wanting to their own revenge, as, by frequently making a stand, they slaughtered their pursuers in heaps ... they drove down the Normans, when roused with indignation ... into the valley beneath, where, easily hurling their javelins and rolling down stones on them ... they destroyed them to a man ... first one party conquering and then another, prevailed as long as the life of Harold continued; but when he fell from having his brain pierced with an arrow, the flight of the English ceased not until night. (B. Thorpe, *Ancient Laws and Institutes of England.* London: Eyre and Spotiswoode, 1840, p. 53)

The Battle of Hastings marked the end of Anglo-Saxon rule of the island kingdom, and the beginning of the Norman occupation.

Alfred the Great

849-899

Personal Background

Family. Alfred was one of four boys and brother of one girl, the children of a king in England. Born about 849 in Berkshire in southern Great Britain, he descended from a long line of Saxon kings. His grandfather, King Egbert, had named England in 827. He called it Angle-land, land of the people called Angles. Alfred's father was Ethelwulf, who ruled as the king of Wessex. Alfred's mother, Osburga, was the queen but had no official power or claim to the throne.

Rome. Though born into the royal family, it was unlikely that Alfred would succeed his father as king. He was the fourth oldest son. Nevertheless, he was sent on a pilgrimage to Rome at age four to be blessed by the pope as a future Saxon leader. Pope Leo IV treated young Alfred as his own "spiritual son" and made him an honorary consul of Rome (Mapp, p. 24). Alfred stayed with the pope at the Vatican court for at least one year and perhaps a second.

Rome, one of the largest and most diverse European cities, was considered in the ninth century to be the "capital of the civilized world" (Mapp, p. 24). The Coliseum and Pantheon still stood, the arts—drama, literature, philosophy, and music—flourished, and the streets were filled with European, Mediterranean, North African, Near and Far Eastern faces. Coming from the

▲ **Alfred the Great**

Event: Viking invasion of Britain.

Role: During an era of near-constant war in England between the Vikings and Anglo-Saxons, Alfred the Great, King of the West Saxons achieved a fifteen-year peace with the Vikings and rebuilt both his military power and the Anglo-Saxon culture. One of the most beloved leaders in history, Alfred translated books from Latin to English and encouraged Anglo-Saxon literature.

rural countryside of Wessex where he had only likely been exposed to Anglo-Saxon nobility and farmers, Alfred was deeply impressed by Rome. As an adult he regarded his stay there as an important part of his education, where he developed an appreciation of other cultures and realized that the center of government could also be the center of learning, as it was at the Vatican court.

While his father was responsible for Alfred's knowledge of commerce and politics, it was his mother who is credited with developing his interest in reading and learning. According to legend, she acquired one of the few books of Anglo-Saxon poems. There was not much literature in print in the languages of either the Angles or Saxons, and the Anglo-Saxon language was still growing into a widely accepted standard form. Still, Osburha offered this prize to the first of her sons who could learn to read it. The story goes that Alfred won over his three older brothers. It was not until he was an adult, however, that he would master the formal language in which most Western literature was published, Latin.

Born into conflict. Alfred grew up during a time of war between the Anglo-Saxons and Vikings. The first Viking attacks on the British Isles began in 793 and had drastically increased by 850. Before the ninth century, the Vikings typically raided the land for a few months, loading hoards of silver and gold coins and jewels onto their large Viking ships. They then returned to Scandinavia with their newfound wealth.

However, by 850, the Viking tactics had changed. In the winter of 850-51, they set up camp for the first time in the British Isles and made clear their intentions of conquering the land. No longer content to plunder and flee, the Vikings were now intent on settling in Great Britain.

Torch passed. When eight-year-old Alfred returned from Rome with his father, he found his life dramatically changed. His mother had died, and his father had remarried a very young French woman named Judith. The marriage caused a scandal in Wessex and Ethelwulf was forced to turn his authority over to his eldest son, Ethelbald. Ethelwulf died shortly thereafter and within four years so did Ethelbald. The kingdom next went to Ethelbert, the second son, but amid constant Viking attack, he was wounded

▲ Medieval falconers; Alfred the Great learned the skills he would need to become a future West Saxon king, including falconry, military strategy, and how to fight with broadswords and daggers.

and died in 866. Ethelred, the third son, became king and Alfred, now seventeen, served as his chief general. Alfred had been taught by his brothers the skills he would need to become a strong person and a future West Saxon king. He learned hunting, fishing, falconry, military strategy, and how to fight with broadswords and daggers. Though it is clear Alfred possessed a fine memory—often listening to and reciting Anglo-Saxon epics such as *Beowulf*—it is unlikely that he was taught to read and write beyond the most basic level.

First tests of manhood. From age seventeen to twenty-two, Alfred joined his brother and countrymen in fighting against the Vikings, who were gaining ground throughout Great Britain. By 871 the Vikings controlled nearly all of East Anglia, York, and Nottingham, and had captured the powerful cities of London and Canterbury. They were threatening to take Wessex—the last stronghold of the Saxons—when Alfred scored his first major military victory at White Horse Hill. There followed a second victory at Morton but with a great price: Ethelred was killed. At age twenty-two, Alfred became king of the West Saxons.

Participation: Viking Invasion of Britain

Year of Battles. The first year of Alfred's reign, 871, was marked by such fierce fighting that historians called it the "the year of battles" (Wilson, p. 58). During this troubled year, Alfred personally fought in nine separate battles before he was able to secure a cease-fire in 872. He agreed to pay the Vikings and let them retain the territories they had already acquired in exchange for keeping Wessex under Saxon rule. With this agreement, Alfred gained three peaceful years, during which time he rebuilt his war-torn army.

Eddington. By 876 the Vikings were again on the attack near Wessex, led by Danish King Guthrum. Though Alfred had begun building England's first navy and had refortified his army, many of his men were tired from nearly twenty years of constant war. When the Vikings invaded Wessex in January 878, most of Alfred's army gave in to defeat and deserted their king. Alfred was able to escape with a small band of loyal soldiers into the woods in Somerset. Most of his people thought he was dead.

Four months Alfred hid, surrounded by his enemies and faced with certain defeat. But somehow he once again was able to rebuild his army. He emerged from hiding in May 878 with a substantial force of men and scored a miraculous victory against

Epic Tales

An "epic" tale is a long heroic poem that describes the bravery and accomplishments of a great legendary leader. These poems, of which *Beowulf* is the best-known Anglo-Saxon example, were told aloud by "bards" or "scops" in mead halls (much like modern-day taverns), often accompanied by a harp or lute. Epics described the "heroic ideal" or code of chivalry, in which loyalty to one's country or kingdom was the truest measure of manhood. These epics had great influence on Anglo-Saxon culture. The epic hero was the ideal man in the eyes of the Anglo-Saxon.

▲ Alfred the Great depicted on a silver coin of his reign. Alfred commanded cultural and social reforms that made him one of the most loved leaders in British history.7

Guthrum at Eddington. Impressed by his courageous stand and stunning victory, Guthrum surrendered. Alfred, a very religious man, insisted he owed his victory to God and convinced Guthrum to be baptized in the Christian faith. Formerly pagan as were most Vikings, Guthrum converted to Christianity and was given East Anglia to govern as a peaceful ally. Alfred now regained control of the rest of England.

Massive reform. For the following twenty years, Alfred commanded the cultural and social reforms that have made him one of the most loved leaders in British history. First, he allied the Scandinavians and Saxons through law and established friendly relations between the two very similar cultures. He next turned his attention to rebuilding the Saxon army, constructing a formidable navy, and fortifying cities. Learning from the Vikings, Alfred built England's first major fleet of ships and fortressed cities such as London to guard against future sea invasion.

Between 893 and 897 there were again attacks by Vikings—this time from Normandy, in present-day northern France. But Alfred's military, now better armed and prepared to combat against sea invasion, ultimately drove the invaders back. With a strong military in place and cities relatively secured, Alfred now concentrated on restoring the "soul" of England.

Alfred and England's education. From his childhood experiences in Rome, Alfred had learned that a king could better direct than defend and could create the laws of his country. He could also stimulate social and cultural change. Alfred had a deep interest in education, the arts, and religion and felt it was his moral obligation to educate his subjects.

After enacting a code of laws and creating a trial-by-jury system, Alfred began his and the nation's education. He gave half his income to churches and monasteries throughout the world and recruited monks and scholars to teach in England. He was among the first to learn to read and write in Latin and English, or in those days *Englisc*. The old English had been at first only a spoken language, *Englisc spraec*. Not until the West Saxon king before Alfred, Egbert, were serious efforts made to unify the language and make a common written form. All the world's major literary, religious, and philosophical works were written in Latin. Alfred used his own knowledge to translate books into English. His efforts to translate the great literature of his day into English, as well as to record Anglo-Saxon prose in English, helped preserve those works and encouraged its future development.

In one of his most far-reaching efforts, Alfred established schools throughout England and was the first leader to call for national education. Previously, only a few of the nobility were educated. Alfred sought to end illiteracy and ignorance and, "like a productive bee," he began "pollinating the masses" with knowledge (Honeyman, p. 76).

Alfred encouraged the writing of the *Anglo-Saxon Chronicle,* an annual newspaper detailing the daily life and history of the Anglo-Saxons in England. Because of Alfred's efforts, Anglo-Saxon literature and history, which was previously unwritten, was recorded on paper and survives to this day.

Aftermath

For the last four years of his life, Alfred divided his time between prayer and scholarship. He continued to translate books, adding his own introductions and insights to many of the works, and spent four to eight hours a day in church. Alfred died at age fifty on October 26, 899, after suffering from frequent illness most of his life. He was survived by his wife of thirty years, Elswitha, three daughters, Ethelflaeda, Ethelgeda, and Elfrida, and two sons, Edward, and Ethelward. Edward, the eldest son, succeeded his father as king.

> **Major Books Translated by Alfred**
>
> Bede's *Ecclesiastical History of the World*
> Boetheus's *Consolation of Philosophy*
> Gregory the Great's *Pastoral Care*

Alfred strove to live his life "in a becoming manner, and at my death to leave to those who follow me a worthy memorial in my work" (Honeyman, p. 68). He certainly accomplished those goals and at his death was mourned worldwide. In a time in history filled with war and conflict, Alfred's achievements were amazing and far-reaching. As the writer Johann Gottfried Herder said, Alfred's life served as "a pattern for kings in a time of extremity, a bright star in the history of mankind" (Honeyman, p. 94).

For More Information

Honeyman, A. Van Doren. *Alfred the Great.* Plainfield, New Jersey: Honeyman and Co. 1905.

Linklater, Eric. *The Conquest of England.* New York: Doubleday, 1966.

Mapp, Alf J. *The Golden Dragon.* La Salle, Illinois: Open Court, 1974.

Magnusson, Magnus. *Vikings!* New York: E. P. Dutton, 1980.

Wilson, David M., and others. *The Vikings in England.* London: Anglo-Danish Viking Project, 1981.

Canute the Great

c. 995-1035

Personal Background

Early life. Canute (also known as Cnut or Knud) was born in approximately 995 in Jelling, Jutland, Denmark. The son of Danish Viking king Sweyn I Forkbeard and Queen Gunhild, Canute grew up during the height of the Viking age (793-1066). Under his father's rule, Denmark had become the most powerful and richest Scandinavian nation. The Danes had the largest naval fleet in the North Seas, a thriving economy based on international trade, and were threatening to conquer England.

King Sweyn's dream. Beginning the same year his son was born, Sweyn led attacks on Great Britain, hopeful of making it part of his growing Danish empire. By July 1014 he was within a year of realizing his goal. With eighteen-year-old Canute at his side, Sweyn set sail for England with a large fleet of Viking warriors. They were going to take the island once and for all. Governed by King Ethelred, England was not well organized. There was fighting within the government, the Anglo-Saxons lacked a central command for its military, and, as always, the island was very vulnerable to sea invasion because of its long coastline. Though **Alfred the Great** (849-901; see entry) had begun to build England's navy and had fortified many coastal cities during his reign, in the hundred years since his death little else had been done to improve England's defenses, and constant Viking attacks

▲ Canute the Great

Event: Viking invasion of Britain.

Role: Danish Viking leader Canute the Great conquered England in 1016 and in 1028 became the first to rule a united North Sea empire that included Denmark, England, Scotland, the Shetland and Orkney Islands, and Norway. King for twenty years, Canute is best known for bringing peace, unity, and stability to the previously divided and war-torn North Sea region.

had severely weakened the military. Further, Ethelred was not the popular ruler that Alfred had been and, as a result, loyalties were divided throughout the country. All these conditions made England an easy target for the Viking invaders.

Knowing this, Sweyn struck the west coast with a powerful fleet of ships and overwhelmed the countryside. He won immediate submission of the people with little or no bloodshed. Ethelred fled to Normandy (in northern France) with his family and, in his absence, Sweyn, though not formally crowned, became king.

A kingdom comes and goes. Sweyn became the first to rule both Denmark and England but his long-awaited dream was short-lived. Five weeks after his stunning victory he died, on February 3, 1014. It appeared that Canute would inherit the English throne at the age of nineteen years, but the Anglo-Saxons had other intentions. Because of Canute's young age and inexperience as a leader and warrior, the English had little faith in him. Realizing his weakness, they sent for Ethelred in Normandy to mount an army and reclaim the English throne. Advised of the situation, Canute decided to return to Denmark where he could refortify his troops and plan a second invasion.

But before leaving the British Isles, Canute exacted a small revenge. His father had taken some Anglo-Saxon prisoners, who were kept in Sandwich. Before releasing them, Canute had their ears, noses, and hands cut off in a display of anger and force. He left Britain largely disliked because of his action but showed that he would not be turned away lightly. This would not be the last England had seen of Canute.

Participation: Viking Invasion of Britain

A warrior's education. In Denmark Canute organized forces and planned to recapture Great Britain. Troops were refortified and a fleet of Viking warships was assembled. Eirik of Hladir, one of the most experienced warriors of his day, and Thorkell the Tall, also a very experienced Viking who had fought extensively in England, joined Canute and became his *eaxlgestealla* or shoulder-companions. Canute was very fortunate to have these two men at his side. From them he would get the guidance as well as the strength and leadership he needed to defeat the Anglo-Saxons.

Canute's war. In the summer of 1015, with a powerful fleet of two hundred ships, Canute set sail for England just as his father had done the year before. Again, the Danes attacked the west coast of England and, again, they were victorious. Canute showed that he had learned from his father and "shoulder-companions" and was becoming a respected and talented leader.

Ethelred had not regained total power since his restoration to the throne. His forces were ineffective against the crush of Viking invaders. He died amid the fighting and his son, Edmund Ironside, became king. Edmund proved to be a much more formidable opponent than his father. About the same age as Canute, Edmund succeeded in recapturing Wessex when the Danes moved east toward London. But at the battle of Essex, facing Canute's forces head-on, Edmund was defeated. When Essex fell, Canute won the war and claimed the title of King of England. However, because of his bravery in battle, Edmund gained Canute's respect. Canute allowed Edmund to retain rule of Wessex, while he took control of Mercia and the Danelaw.

King Canute and the birth of a North Sea empire. By 1017 Edmund had died and Canute, age twenty-two, was

▲ **Battle array characteristic of the Viking Anglo-Saxon period. The weapons carried were the bronze-hilted sword and a battle axe.**

the undisputed king of England. He soon married Ethelred's widow, Emma. This allied him closely to the English nobility and the government of Normandy across the English Channel. Duke

Richard II of Normandy was Emma's brother. The marriage—as well as his fair treatment of Edmund Ironside—made him more popular with his subjects. They were inclined to forget the hostage incident of the past.

In 1018 Canute's brother, King Harald of Denmark, died, and Canute inherited the Danish throne. The kingdoms of Denmark and England were officially united under one king for the first time in history. In 1028 Canute added Norway to his empire and also gained control of the Shetland and Orkney Islands and Scotland. Sweden was also closely allied to Canute but retained its own king.

Underrated king. Canute ruled his "North Sea empire" from his court at Winchester, England. Though one of the most underrated leaders of his time, Canute was one of the most successful kings in English history. He brought peace and prosperity to his North Sea empire and tried to uphold the royal traditions of his kingdoms while increasing their wealth and power. He revived old English laws that stressed justice and individual rights. He retained strong ties to the church and, in the tradition of King Alfred, made a pilgrimage to Rome. He was blessed by the pope and made a deal with the Holy Roman Emperor Conrad II to lower trade taxes for his subjects. In England and Europe he built monasteries, churches, and abbeys for nuns and monks. As Canute told his subjects: "I have never spared, nor will I spare in the future, to devote myself and my toil for the need and benefit of my people" (Linklater, p. 139).

The Vikings

Vikings, who came from Sweden, Norway, Denmark, Iceland, and islands of the North Sea and Baltic, were an adventurous lot who built their lives around the sea. Longtime traders of fur, ivory, and amber, the Vikings pioneered the use of skis and skates and built the world's first ships that used both sails and oars. Though their first ventures to new lands were strictly for trade purposes, the Vikings soon became known as fierce warriors and eventually captured and settled territory from Russia to North America. Achieving "word-fame" was the ultimate goal of the Viking warrior, who hoped through acts of bravery and conquest to bring lasting honor to his name and country. Much like the Anglo-Saxons, the Vikings believed that the true test of manhood was to serve one's king valiantly in battle. In fact, most Viking boys became men by going overseas on Viking expeditions and returning with battle experience and riches for their families.

A king's humility. Canute was a considerate and humble ruler who demonstrated his faith in God and his support of Christianity through his generosity. An often-told story illustrates his

▲ Canute commanding the North Sea tide to recede; "Be it known ... that the power of kings is empty and superficial."

humility as king of the North Sea empire. According to legend, Canute had his royal throne carried to the shore of Bosham Beach, where hundreds of his subjects were gathered. When he sat in the throne, he commanded the incoming tide to stop, saying: "The land on which I sit is mine; no one has ever resisted my command.... Therefore I command you not to rise over my land, and not to presume to wet the clothes or limbs of your lord" (Magnusson, p. 275).

Of course the tide did not stop and Canute was soaked with water. The king then looked around to his subjects and said: "Be it known to all inhabitants of the world that the power of kings is empty and superficial, and no one is worthy of the name of king except for Him whose will is obeyed by Heaven, earth, and sea in accordance with eternal laws" (Magnusson, p. 276). He then took off his crown and never wore it again.

Whether the story is fact or myth, a famous picture, the *Liber Vitae* of Hyde Abbey in Winchester, depicts Canute's crown being lifted from his head by an angel who is carrying it to Christ. The story may have grown out of this picture.

Aftermath

Canute's twenty-year reign as king of the North Sea empire ended with his early death at age forty on November 12, 1035. He was buried at Winchester, where most previous kings of England were laid to rest.

Though little is known about Canute's personal life, his success as a leader is well recorded. His major accomplishment was uniting the North Sea empire and bringing a long and much-needed peace to the region. Under Canute's rule, the North Sea kingdom was the "largest, richest, and most unified state of its time in northwestern Europe" (Wilson, p. 165).

Canute's son, Harthacnut (Haroldcanute), succeeded his father as king of England, but within two years he was forced to give up the crown to Edward, exiled son of Ethelred the Unready. Harthacnut managed to keep the crown of Denmark but the North Sea empire was no longer strong and united. Canute's control of the empire was an amazing individual accomplishment. He alone had the strength—personally and militarily—to keep his vast kingdom intact and at peace. His death signaled the end of the empire and the re-emergence of wars among the peoples of northern Europe.

Canute's Word-Fame

Many epics were written about Canute by Scandinavians, giving him the lasting "word-fame" most Vikings hoped to achieve. In *Knytlinga Saga* he was described as tall, strong, fair-haired, keen-eyed, bountiful, valiant, and all-conquering. Clearly, as the story of his life illustrates, "He was a man of great good luck in everything to do with power" (Jones, p. 373).

For More Information

Jones, Gwyn. *A History of the Vikings.* London: Oxford University Press, 1968.

Lawson, M. K. *Canute*. London: Longman Group UK, 1993.

Linklater, Eric. *The Conquest of England*. Garden City, New York: Doubleday, 1966.

Magnusson, Magnus. *Vikings!*. New York: E.P. Dutton, 1980.

Wilson, David M. *The Vikings in England*. London: Anglo-Danish Viking Project, 1981.

William the Conqueror

c. 1028-1087

Personal Background

Birth. William the Conqueror was born around 1028 in Falaise, France. He was the illegitimate child of Herleve, daughter of a local tanner, and Duke Robert I of Normandy. He was often referred to by his detractors as William the Bastard.

William was from a long line of Viking leaders, or "Northmen," who had come from Scandinavia and settled in France in the tenth century. His great-great-grandfather, Hrolf—better known as Rollo—founded the duchy of Normandy in 911. By the time William was born, his family had ruled the French province for 150 years.

Duke of Normandy. In 1035 William's father went on a pilgrimage to Jerusalem and never returned. At age eight William succeeded his father as Duke of Normandy. Like the dukes before him, William inherited powerful enemies. Violence and fighting had marked the government of Normandy since its establishment. Threats were continually made against William's family from barons within and rivals outside of Normandy. When William succeeded his father at such a young age, he became a prime target of attack. During his first years as duke, all of William's closest advisers were killed and an attempt was even made on William's life.

Personal life. William was described as "massive" and "impressive," with the "strength and gauntness of an alpine crag"

▲ William the Conqueror

Event: Norman invasion of England.

Role: In 1066 William the Conqueror led a massive invasion of Great Britain, defeated King Harold Godwinsson at the battle of Hastings, and became the first Norman king of England. His conquest of the English throne signaled the end of the Viking Age.

(Brooke, p. 173). Though he ruled by fear and to many seemed almost "inhuman," he cultivated a lifelong relationship with one of the wisest scholars of his day, "father of the monks" Lanfranc, whom William had installed as archbishop in England. William also risked expulsion from the church for his marriage to his wife, Matilda, a union the pope opposed for political reasons. William appears to have been a passionate man, driven to seek the English throne. He was also an illiterate soldier who loved hunting and the outdoors. William was raised Christian and as king of England built many stone abbeys and castles that remain to this day.

The Vikings in Normandy

First called "Northmandy," Normandy, today a province of France, derives its name from the "Northmen" who were given the land in 911. Norwegian Viking Hrolf, better known as Rollo, led one of the frequent raids into France. When Paris came into danger, the king of France offered the Normandy area in exchange for the freedom of Paris. The first Duke of Normandy and his family ruled the province in alliance with the King of France, Charles III, through the tenth century (Magnusson, p. 282-83).

William and Matilda were married for thirty-eight years and had three sons, Robert, William, and Henry.

Power and fear. Growing up with constant threats to his life, William learned very early to defend himself. He became a soldier; learned to fight with bow and arrow, the war axe, and the broadsword; and learned military strategy. William saw the violence around him and became convinced that in order to retain power a leader had to be feared. He did his best to strengthen his army and become a fierce ruler.

From 1047 to 1054 William was engaged in near-constant warfare. Finally, by age thirty, he conquered his local enemies, including King Henry I of France, whom he drove from the region, and established himself as the undisputed ruler of Normandy. With his home country now at peace, William could turn his attentions across the English Channel to his next goal: he could begin planning the Norman invasion of England.

A promise and an idea. Edward the Confessor, son of English King Ethelred the Unready, grew up as an exile in Normandy. During that time, he and William became friends. When Edward was recalled to the English throne in 1042, their friendship remained intact, and in 1051 William paid Edward a state visit.

▲ **Great Britain; had it not been for the wind blowing in an unfavorable
direction, William would have crossed the English Channel in August
and faced the full force of Harold Godwinsson's army.**

According to William, Edward—who may have already known he
was dying—asked William to be his successor as king. Perhaps
because of his childhood in Normandy, Edward seemed partial to
the Normans and may have preferred a Norman to succeed him

209

rather than Harold Godwinsson, a descendent of Danish Vikings who was next in line to the throne. Whatever the case, from that day on William firmly claimed he had a right to the English throne.

Rivals meet. In 1064 William's main rival to the English throne, Harold Godwinsson, paid him an odd and unexpected visit. Whether he was blown off-course by the wind or intended to cross the English Channel to Normandy is unclear. What is certain is that he became a guest of William's at his official residence in Normandy. William treated Harold like visiting royalty, took him on a tour of the countryside, and even had him knighted. In return for his "hospitality," William made Harold swear an oath of loyalty: he was to promise to help William become king of England. Harold agreed but later said he was forced to swear allegiance and would not honor his commitment. Harold himself became king of England on January 6, 1066, one day after Edward died.

Participation: Norman Invasion of England

Surprise attack. When Harold Godwinsson became king, William decided to invade England and take the throne (which he felt was rightfully his) by force. However, as he built his army and fortified his fleet, a third leader was also plotting an attack.

Norwegian King Harald Hardradi attacked the north coast of England in the summer of 1066, with nine thousand men and a fleet of three hundred ships. Harold of England had been expecting an invasion, but from Normandy rather than Norway. He was caught off-guard by the unexpected Viking attack from the north. His troops were stationed facing the English Channel that separated England and France. By the end of September, Harold, to his credit, had moved them across the country to face the northern foe at the battle of Stamford Bridge. Though Hardradi had the upper hand and appeared to be defeating Harold's forces, he made a tactical error that cost him the war and his life. He anchored his ships too far from the battleground and could not get reinforcements in time. He was killed by an arrow to the chest on September 25, 1066, and Harold defeated his troops.

A strange ally. While the war in England raged between the two kings, William was preparing to cross the channel. Armed

▲ Manuscript illumination depicting the death of Harold Godwinsson at
the hands of William the Conqueror during the Battle of Hastings.

with seven hundred ships and ten thousand men, he sat perched
at the shores of Normandy waiting for the wind to change to a
favorable direction. Had it not been for that wind, he would have
attacked England in August and faced the full force of Harold's
army lined along the shore, awaiting his arrival. However, the

wind kept him in port until after Hardradi's invasion. On September 28, when Harold's army was safely across the country, the wind finally changed directions. William set sail for Pevensey Beach with his huge invasion fleet. He landed without incident about ten miles from the port town of Hastings.

Battle of Hastings. Though wartorn and hundreds of miles away, Harold's army made it to London by October 5. Harold had learned of William's landing and hoped to trap his forces at Pevensey Beach for the winter. However, the Normans were moving too fast and met Harold's army in Hastings on October 14, 1066. The battle was fierce. William commanded his forces while Harold led his. Infantry, cavalry, and archers fought on foot and horseback with axes, bows and arrows, and heavy swords. Though the soldiers wore heavy chainmail and metal helmets and carried shields made of metal and hide, hundreds were killed by axe and arrow. It was in this "arrow-storm" that Harold finally died, either struck by an arrow in the eye or hewn down by a Norman knight. When Harold fell, so did England. William the Conqueror became the first Norman king of England on Christmas Day 1066, and the Viking Age officially came to an end. A one-day battle had changed the direction of the government of England.

A Record of the Conquest of England

The Bayeux Tapestry is an extraordinary embroidered needlework that depicts the Norman Conquest and Battle of Hastings (from the Norman point of view). Forty meters by fifty centimeters, the tapestry that resembles a modern-day political cartoon was produced at the famous needlework school in Canterbury. It was commissioned in 1066 by William's half-brother, Bishop Odo, and currently hangs in the Old Archbishop's Palace at Bayeux in Normandy (Magnusson, p. 307).

Aftermath

William ruled England for twenty-one years and established a lasting Norman dynasty. The descendants of the "Northmen" had succeeded where their countrymen had failed. Now William found that he had taken charge of a very loosely knit kingdom. Nobles known as earls had been granted large pieces of land in exchange for support of the old English kings. These earls had become powerful and no longer felt obligated to provide an endless parade of knights for the king's protection. William had had troubles with

▲ A scene from the Bayeux Tapestry depicting the English fleeing the Battle of Hastings.

the nobles of Normandy and was prepared to change England. He broke the large fiefs into smaller ones in order to make the earls more dependent on the central government. Some of these smaller land grants were given to William's friends from Normandy. He made everyone, even the serfs who worked the land, subjects directly responsible to him, thus building a peasant class from which he could call soldiers in time of need.

Then, in 1085 and 1086, William called for a survey such as had never been made before. His workers counted and recorded everything in England:

> So very narrowly did he cause the survey to be made that there was not a single hide nor a rood of land, nor—it is shameful to relate that which he thought no shame to do—was there an ox or a cow or a pig passed by that was not set down in the accounts. (Cheyney, p. 112)

The survey provided later readers with an accurate account of the environment, wealth, and daily lives of the people of William's time. It is know as the *Doomsday Survey.*

Thus William spent his time as ruler making sure that he would leave a well-organized England, governed by a strong central government that watched over the environment with a system of local governors and enforcers, the sheriffs made famous by such stories as *Robin Hood*.

England after William. All three of William's sons became Norman rulers, either in Normandy or England. The oldest son, Robert, had broken with his father. Therefore, when William died on September 9, 1087, at age sixty, his second son, William Rufus, ascended the throne of England. He is known as "the worst king that has ever occupied the throne of England" (Brooke, p. 176). Robert took the second prize and became Duke of Normandy. Henry later became King Henry I of England.

For More Information

Brooke, Christopher. *The Saxon and Norman Kings.* London: B. T. Batsford, 1963.

Cheyney, E. P. *Readings in English History Drawn from the Original Sources.* Boston, Massachusetts: Ginn, 1908.

Douglas, David C. *William the Conqueror.* Berkeley: University of California Press, 1964.

Magnusson, Magnus. *Vikings!* New York: E. P. Dutton, 1980.

Bibliography

Benjamin, Samuel G. *The Story of Persia*. New York: Gordon Press, 1977.

Brodsky, Alyn. *The Kings Depart*. New York: Harper, 1974.

Browne, Edward. *Literary History of Persia*. 4 vols. Cambridge, England: Cambridge University Press, 1930.

Cameron, Averil. *The Later Roman Empire*. Cambridge, Massachusetts: Harvard University Press, 1993.

Cooley, John K. *Baal, Christ and Mohammed: Religion and Revolution in North Africa*. New York: Holt, Rinehardt and Winston, 1965.

Dodds, E. R. *Pagan and Christian in an Age of Anxiety*. New York: Norton, 1970.

The Encyclopedia of Islam. London: Luzac, 1960.

Garraty, John A., and Peter Gray, editors. *The Columbia History of the World*. New York: Dorset, 1972.

Giles, Herbert A. *A History of Chinese Literature*. New York: Frederick Ungar, 1963.

Goldstein, Jonathan A., translator. *First Maccabees*. Garden City, New York: Doubleday, 1976.

Graetz, Heinrich. *History of the Jews*. Vol. 1. Philadelphia: Jewish Publication Society of America, 1891.

Hart, Henry Hirsch. *Poems of the Hundred Names: A Short Introduction to Chinese Poetry*. Stanford, California: Stanford University Press, 1954.

Hirsh, Marilyn. *The Hanukkah Story*. New York: Bonim, 1977.

Hogarth, David G. *Arabia*. 1922. Reprint: New York: Hyperion, 1985.

Hourani, Albert. *A History of the Arab Peoples*. Cambridge, Massachusetts: Belknap Press, 1991.

Kiernan, Thomas. *The Arabs: Their History, Aims, and Challenge to the Industrialized World*. Boston, Massachusetts: Little, Brown, 1975.

Lang, David Marshall, editor. *Guide to Eastern Literature*. New York: Praeger, 1971.

Norwich, John Julius. *Byzantium: The Early Centuries*. London: Penguin Books, 1990.

Nutting, Anthony. *The Arabs: A Narrative History from Mohammed to the Present*. New York: C. N. Potter, 1968.

Patai, Raphael. *The Arab Mind*. New York: Scribner's, 1973.

Pearlman, Moshe. *The Maccabees*. New York: Macmillan, 1973.

Perry, R. C., editor. *A History of Christianity: Readings on the History of Early and Medieval Christianity*. Englewood Cliffs, New Jersey: Prentice-Hall, 1962.

BIBLIOGRAPHY

Rexroth, Kenneth. *One Hundred Poems from the Chinese.* New York: New Directions, 1959.

Roelof, Roolvick. *Historical Atlas of the Muslim Peoples.* Amsterdam: Djambatam, 1957.

Salibi, Kamal S. *History of Arabia.* New York: Caravan, 1980.

Sarson, Mary, and Mabel Addison Phillips. *The History of the People of Israel in Pre-Christian Times.* London: Longmans, Green, 1912.

Silver, Daniel Jeremy. *A History of Judaism.* New York: Basic Books, 1974.

Spielvogel, Jackson J. *Western Civilization.* 2nd edition. St. Paul, Minnesota: West, 1994.

Wells, H. W. *Six Sanskrit Plays.* Bombay: Asia Publishing House, 1964.

Williams, J. A., editor. *Themes of Islamic Civilization.* Berkeley, California: University of California Press, 1971.

Wollaston, A. N. *The Sword of Islam.* London: John Murray, 1905.

Index

Bold indicates entries and their page numbers; (ill.) indicates illustrations.

$\mathscr{P}$ROFILES IN WORLD HISTORY

Significant Events and the People

Who Shaped Them

Volume 5: *British World Influence to Seeking Alternatives to Capitalism, 1750-1900*

Volume 6: *Social Reform to World Wars, 1880-1945*